DOORS INTO LIFE
Through Five Devotional Classics

Douglas V. Steere

DOORS
INTO LIFE

Through Five Devotional Classics

By **DOUGLAS V. STEERE**

PROFESSOR OF PHILOSOPHY
IN HAVERFORD COLLEGE

HARPER & BROTHERS
PUBLISHERS
NEW YORK

To
E. M. S.
With Affection

CONTENTS

Introduction

INTRODUCTION

THIS little book is in the nature of an attempt to make a token interest payment on a debt. The debt is a very personal one. For the five devotional books which are the focus of attention here have been doors into life for me, and the personalities behind them have exerted a continual drawing power.

There is an old Quaker phrase which can best express what these books do to me. They "speak to my condition." The *Imitation of Christ* lays bare the cross and keeps it bare; the *Introduction to the Devout Life* is a book of nursery exercises for a nursery-school beginner in private prayer and in the agile service of God; John Woolman's *Journal* unites the life of prayer and worship and social concern and is a never-ending renewer of the faith that Jesus meant us to take literally the words of the Lord's Prayer: "Thy kingdom come, thy will be done *on earth* as it is in heaven"; *Purity of Heart* is the ax that is laid at the root of the barren fig tree to remind it that after the reprieve that was granted it to permit of one more dunging, if there is still no fruit, it will be removed; von Hügel's *Letters* are a witness to the great health of the religious life that embraces every phase of our being: the mind, the will, the emotions, as embodied in the sweep of affection and concern of this noble Christian.

These books span six centuries and have sprung from

widely separated religious confessions: the *Imitation* from the new devotional movement of late fourteenth-century Dutch Christianity; the *Introduction* from the sixteenth and early seventeenth-century Catholic Renaissance; Woolman's *Journal* from colonial American Quakerism; *Purity of Heart* from nineteenth-century Scandinavian Lutheranism; and von Hügel's *Letters* from a Roman Catholic thinker of our own century whose influence on Anglo-Saxon Protestant thought was exceeded by no one in his generation. Yet they rise above their centuries and above their confessions in the universal authority with which they speak to our condition today.

Here and there in these books, practices are commended to the reader which will grate upon his sensibilities because they are not common to his own tradition or because they are dated by the century in which the book was written. But if he has even a flicker of ecumenical charity he will go on reading and on the next page he is likely to find a word that seems especially meant for him. T. S. Eliot's remark that we may find companions in men of other centuries who are nearer to us than most of our own contemporaries is likely to be personally experienced by more than a few as they read one or the other of these books.

It is almost impossible to separate a great devotional book from its author, for it reflects so personally what he has discovered and what he is willing to share with others. Therefore in these studies biography and discussion of the book and of its contents flow freely back and forth into each other. There are two excellent little books that have encouraged me in preparing this one. Gaius Glenn Atkins' *Pilgrims of the Lonely Road,* which was written in the second decade of this century, and Willard Sperry's *Strangers and Pilgrims,* which appeared ten years ago. If there is any difference of approach to be found here, it is in an attempt to present in these chapters not only the setting of the book and some reflections on its significance, but to communicate as well the central core of the message of each book as it is singled out for attention. And to this end, I have often let the authors speak for themselves. Yet at bottom the goal is the same: to encourage others to make the reading of the originals a part of the practice of each day's life. To do this, however, one must own them and mark them up and have them at his side. Happily all but one of the books mentioned are readily available.[1]

The substance of the first three and the fifth chapters of this book have been given as the Carew Lectures at Hartford Theological Seminary in February, 1945 and under the Hoyt lectureship at Union Theological Seminary in June, 1947. The privilege of revising these lectures and of adding the fourth chapter has been given me by Haverford College during a generous time of sabbatical leave. During this period my wife and I have been most graciously lodged as guests of the Sigtuna Foundation at their guesthouse in Sigtuna, Sweden. For the encouragement of these lecture-ships and for the hospitality of each of these occasions, I want especially to thank acting-President Alexander Purdy, Professor William Davidson and Rektor Ingmar Sahlin. My wife has helped me constantly in revising these lectures and

[1] *Imitation of Christ* is obtainable in the Everyman Ed. or in either the full or pocket edition edited by Klein and published by Harper & Brothers.

Introduction to the Devout Life is at present only accessible in the edition published by Pustet, Philadelphia.

The *Journal* of John Woolman (Whittier ed.) can be secured for $1.25 through the Friends Bookstore, 304 Arch St., Philadelphia, Pa.

Purity of Heart is available in the new revised edition published by Harper & Brothers.

in seeing them through the stages of publication, and our friend Howard Lutz has again helped us with the proofs. They both know how inadequate are any expressions of my gratitude.

DOUGLAS V. STEERE

Sigtuna Foundation,
Sigtuna, Sweden.
March 1, 1948.

I

The *Imitation of Christ*

CHAPTER 1

The *Imitation of Christ*

WE LIVE in a season when the prospects for the Christian religion in the Western world seem grim indeed. Secularism, which is the living of life as though God were dead, as though He did not exist, has gone so far in Europe that even the mask of being Christian states has been dropped in country after country.

In ourselves, the seeds of the same mood that has brought this about daily become more and more evident. We see this secularist mood growing in education, in marriage, in the family, and even in the most intimate presuppositions of personal life. In public affairs we see it at work de-personalizing our sense of responsibility for our neighbors and delegating this responsibility to impersonal concentrations of public power which make decisions with little or no reference to the life or law of God.

The French writer Georges Bernanos left France after the 1938 affair at Munich and with his family settled in self-exile on a back country farm in Brazil. In France's darkest hour of humiliation in 1941, he wrote a public letter to his fellow countrymen in which he warned them to beware of the inward life of their ultimate liberators, England and America:

Too late it will be understood that the totalitarian regimes had only travelled the same road in a few years, as the realist materialist democracies were to travel in a century or two. . . . What the dictators wanted to do in a few years will be accomplished in fifty or a hundred; but the result will be the same; the state will have conquered everything, seduced everything, absorbed everything.

And the state which Bernanos refers to is not a state bound to Christian principles.

This secularism pours in over the private and public life of our time like the salt water of the North Sea pouring in through the breached dikes on the island of Walcheren, sterilizing the soil that seven centuries of the costliest labor had succeeded in reclaiming. It is this which we who care for the Christian cause would do well to note. For those who have on their shoulders the responsibility for sharing the fellowship of Christ with the generation ahead cannot presume to have sweet soil to cultivate. They will have to contend with bitterness and hatred and rancor and a relapse into a mad passion for an irresponsible material security bought at almost any price. Christian values of love, and generosity, and tolerance, and pity, and humility will be laughed to scorn. Gandhi will not be the only one to suffer assassination. Such a period will call for a deeper dedication than the more settled times of the past few generations have demanded, and will reach out for men of firmer stuff in positions of Christian leadership. I always remember what the American representative, Gouverneur Morris wrote back from Paris to George Washington, referring to King Louis XVI: "He was a good man. In ordinary times he would have made a good king. But he has inherited a revolution."

In times such as these, God can use as his servants only men and women who can be trusted to be loyal to the core to Him and to His cause. This is a kind of loyalty no congressional committee can ever ascertain. Its springs are too hidden ever to be fully determined. Even the person himself may not be sure of his own faith because he is all too aware of his own frailty and weakness. Over the centuries this loyalty to God has been called devotion, and it is a good name and we might well keep it. For devotion, which is a derivative of the Latin word for *to vow*, means to yield oneself, to commit oneself, to consecrate oneself to the object of devotion, without regard to the sacrifice or suffering involved.

It is clear that such an attachment cannot be accounted for by the emotions alone, for they are too fluctuating; nor is it any grim clutching of the object by an oaken will; nor is it an exhaustive intellectual grasp of the object by the tentacles of the understanding, although all three of these functions are certainly participants. It seems rather to involve the yielding of a core of our being in which these three functions are all bottomed but none or all of which exhaust it. And this yielding from within seems to have to be done over and over and over again.

It does not belie the fact that Francis of Assisi was soundly converted and that he devoted himself to God before that crucifix in San Damiano at the outset of his religious life, when, at the close of his life, he could gather a few favorite brothers around him and exhort them, "Come, now, let us begin to be Christians." It only reminds us that devotion requires continual nurturing, continual cultivation, continual renewal, continual beginning again, if it is to prepare us for the tasks this generation ahead requires. If this is true, then it is the task of the Christian religion not only to hold constantly before its members the necessity of their yielding themselves continually in acts of devotion to God, but also in encouraging them in the cultivation of these acts.

Learning What to Do with Solitude

I was much impressed as I came across a strikingly relevant passage in the autobiography of the late William I. Sullivan. Dr. Sullivan was a great Free Churchman and Unitarian minister in Germantown, Pennsylvania. He had been educated for the Roman Catholic priesthood and served in it for a decade before the Pope's antimodernist encyclical in 1907 drove him out of the church together with so many other distinguished priests. Speaking late in his life of his own seminary education, he says:

First and foremost came our spiritual cultivation. We were taught the practice of meditation and the first half hour of every day was devoted to it. Besides we made a daily visit to the chapel, which was another period of recollection; and in the evening we listened to spiritual reading for half an hour, usually from the life of a saint, but at certain sessions from a book of formal instruction in the devout life. Then, too, the year of study opened with a week of retreat, and each step in the taking of the various orders of the ministry was preceded by another week of retreat. . . .

It has never failed to give me a sense of dismay to see how many of them [the Protestant seminaries] are content with administering the pedantry of the minister's office to their students leaving almost unnoticed the systematic freshening and fortifying of their souls. There is no species of training that I ever underwent to which I owe more than to the habit of regular periods of inner solitude. Solitary we must be in life's great hours of moral decision; solitary in pain and sorrow; solitary in old age and in going forth at death. Fortunate the man who has learned what to do in solitude and brought himself to see what companionship he may discover in it, what fortitude, what content. By a great blessing, I had an aptitude for these hours of quiet reflection and grew to love them, and with increasing use, I loved them ever more deeply. To be alone and still and thoughtful bestowed upon me the richest joy

I knew; and for this priceless cultivation I shall be thankful always.[1]

William Sullivan may have been unnecessarily disparaging of the concern of Free Church Seminaries in promoting the cultivation of these acts of devotion. There are cells of students in a number of these seminaries whose student members meet regularly in an effort to supply just such nurture. Yet it is probably fair to say that in general the Free Churches, whether with their clergy or their laity, have a kind of reticence about what they might call meddling or tampering with the devotional life of another, and a loathing for anything that smacks of a standardized approach to, or regimentation of, such life. This rugged quality of Protestant individualism has as its hypothesis, however, that the individual is already actively cultivating his own devotional life in his own way. If this surmise is not accurate, then this attitude could become a screen for cowardly lethargy and inaction.

There is also involved in this reticence a presumption that each soul is so utterly unique in its spiritual needs, that it would be a dangerous imposition to confront it with any established practices for the cultivation of its attachment to God. It is doubtful, however, whether after granting that each must find his own form of prayer, his own most helpful devotional aids, the variety is anything like as great as the above presumption implies. And the risk of robbing the soul of an early familiarity with the great classical approaches to prayer and personal discipline—approaches that have supported the lives of some of the greatest characters the Christian world has produced—is a factor that is not to be treated lightly in times when our need is so acute as it is today.

[1] W. I. Sullivan, *Under Orders* (New York: Richard Smith, 1944), p. 49.

Devotional Literature and Its Goal

History has shown that literature that can be classed as devotional is among the most effective stimulants of this life of devotion to God. Again and again it has been the reading and rereading of a devotional book, such as Scupoli's *Spiritual Combat* by Francis de Sales, or *Speculum Perfectionis* by the great Augustine Baker, or William Law's *Serious Call to the Devout Life* by John Wesley, which was decisive in placing the reader's life more firmly in the Divine hands. Jerome Nadal, the eminent follower of Ignatius of Loyola, tells how during his own conversion, Ignatius had instructed him:

He told me to read a chapter of Gerson [the *Imitation of Christ* was at that time attributed to Chancellor Gerson] every day and to meditate on it. It was wonderful how he praised that little book, saying to me that wherever I opened it at random, I would find something suited to the need of the moment as he himself had experienced.[2]

Ignatius lived with "that little book" and a recent biographer records: "We know that for years he read a chapter of the *Imitation of Christ* every day and together with the New Testament, it lay always on the table of his room." [3]

I remember a conversation once with a summer neighbor of mine, Bishop Frederick Leete of the Methodist church, when he told me of a visit that he had made to a young minister's home. While they were talking, the young man was called away to the telephone and there had been an opportunity to scan the books in his library. The Bishop

[2] James Broderick, *The Origin of the Jesuits* (New York: Longman's, 1940), p. 205.

[3] Paul Van Dyke, *Ignatius of Loyola* (New York: Scribner's, 1926), p. 360.

found there almost exclusively current books of religious controversy and among them not a single devotional book that could bring the minister back to his own central commitment and quicken his devotional life. "I could surmise, then and there what that young man was preaching to his people, how he was feeding his congregation and where he would be ten years from then, if he did not change his fodder, and know that my prediction would not fall far of the mark," he quietly added. And I suspect he was right. For the habits we form early and the tools we have ever at hand, whether we are clergy or laity, do much to mark the course of our lives.

At the outset it must be admitted that to one whose taste has been cultivated by modern current periodicals, these devotional classics have a discouraging sameness about them in spite of their particular personal accents. They come back to the same principles that one has heard enunciated as far back as he can remember. There is almost never any new formula for psychological conquest of self or fortune, no new way of swiftly becoming a master of prayer, no short cut to God, no sketch of a simple way by which all the unpleasant personal relations that constantly annoy us could be anesthetized and soothed, no way to be able permanently to look our own unpleasant personal selves in the face and find them as swooningly beautiful as we at moments of sentimental self-adoration, or under the spell of some word of praise, have rather gloried in imagining them to be.

This sameness registers itself in the fact that nearly all of these great books relate themselves to prayer. They lead up to prayer, they make prayer necessary, they almost force us into prayer, and either we leave them or we yield and engage in the practice of private prayer. These books touch upon the areas of life that prayer deals with. They get into the will, into the images that guide the will, into the objects of the emotional attachments of our life, and work upon them. The great ones lead us along either gently or abruptly to consider the exposure of these very inward areas of our life to the scrutiny of God. They increase awareness. They are rare combinations of convicting and of kindling power, convicting us of sin and of the dead areas that need attacking and on the other hand encouraging us and whetting our hunger to abandon ourselves more completely to obedience to God.

A devotional book has back of it a theology, a world view that guides it and there is no intent here to minimize in the least the importance of that world view. One can agree fully with G. K. Chesterton that in choosing a landlady, her world view is more of a guarantee of your future happiness in her boardinghouse than any sample meal or sample housekeeping you may inspect. Yet I have lived in boarding-houses where the good woman's world view left little to be desired but where the application of it left much to be desired. It is at this point that devotional literature so often supplements reading in theology and philosophy, for these works rarely develop the longed-for second volume that deals with applications. After they have shown the reason-ableness of a world view where God exists and where human values and human history are related to his nature, most theologians or philosophers stop. Yet this is just where the religious life begins.

Given such a world, how do I respond to it? How may I come into the deepest personal touch with it? How may I risk my personal destiny in abandonment to that at the heart of it which has been intellectually indicated as acceptable? How may I inwardly participate in the ongoing process of God's life in the world of my time?

These are not specious questions of the sort a scorner once put to Martin Luther when he asked him what God was doing before he created the world. Nor can they be answered by Luther's bright word that God was out in the swamp cutting birch rods to give the man that asked that question an almighty thrashing. They are cries of the heart for help in personal discipline that will implement the permission which the mind has given us to proceed, and they deserve solid help.

To such a cry, a great devotional book speaks plain language. The *Imitation of Christ* contains two classic lines that bring any sentimental or emotional outburst to a full stop before them: "All desire peace, but they do not care for the things that pertain to true peace." [4] "There are many persons who desire the contemplative life, but they will not practice the things which lead to it." [5]

The *Imitation of Christ* quietly goes on to point out that if you really want to share in Christ's life, certain acts of choice are necessary. There is no concealing the writer's belief that where there is no cross in a life there will be no resurrection, or his open admission that the vetoing of certain sweet things causes pain. But if you believe to the point of wanting to follow them, you must discover that faith is not as it has been so often depicted, an act of intellectual mutilation, but that it is rather one of inward abandonment to a course of life that in advance accepts willingly the consequences involved regardless of what they may turn out to be.

Discovering *the* Imitation

I will never forget where I first met the *Imitation of Christ*. I went to spend Christmas week with an Oriel College friend of mine in a suburb of London and as I got into my bed the first night, I found on the bed table one of those

[4] *Imitation of Christ*, III, 25.
[5] *Ibid.*, III, 31.

little courtesies of the truest hospitality, a book. It was the *Imitation of Christ*. I had never seen it before and, as I read in it each night before I went to sleep, I was both drawn to it for its insight into my own condition and repelled by its strangely ascetic tone. Some word of my interest in it led my friend's mother to send it to me after I had left, and I continued in this mixed state toward it during the next two years.

My next discovery was in finding how widely it had been used, that some six thousand editions in all had appeared, and that not only Ignatius of Loyola but as varied a company as Leibniz, Wesley, Kant, General Gordon, Edith Cavell, and Friedrich von Hügel had deeply prized it, and that next to the Bible it was the most widely read devotional book in Christian history. Through Rufus M. Jones' *Studies in Mystical Religion,* I next became interested in the history of mystical movements and began to read of the late fourteenth century Brethren of the Common Life out of which this little book had sprung, and became interested in the possible composite character of the authorship of the *Imitation of Christ.* In this matter of the authorship, Albert Hyma's book, *Christian Renaissance,* as many before it, freely rejected the thesis that the *Imitation* was written by Thomas a Kempis and insisted that a large part of it had come from the writings of the Dutch founder of the order, Gerhard Groote, and other parts from two of the early companions, and that Thomas a Kempis was only the editor. Through this period I tried to follow the shades of the differences of style of the allegedly different authors, and my own copy still is marked up to represent this attempt to follow the analysis which critical scholarship has used upon the Bible as applied to this book of devotion. I cannot say that this period was marked by much devotional profit from the *Imitation,* but it did increase my familiarity with it.

This was followed in 1930 by a week which my wife and I spent at Zwolle in Holland, examining the archives there, with trips to Mt. St. Agnes where a Kempis had lived, to Deventer where Gerhard Groote had founded the original Brethren of the Common Life, and to Windesheim where some remains of the first cloister are still standing. The story of Gerhard Groote and the Brethren of the Common Life which this brief pilgrimage helped to make more vivid for me is well told in Rufus M. Jones' *Studies in Mystical Religion* and his later *Flowering of Mysticism,* as well as in Hyma's *Christian Renaissance,* and needs only a brief sketching here.

Groote and "The Brethren"

Gerhard Groote was a native of Deventer, in Holland. He was wealthy, attractive, and had won brilliant academic honors from Aachen, Paris, Cologne, and Prague. He was a canon lawyer of such standing that at twenty-six he was sent on an important mission to the Pope at Avignon which he completed with conspicuous success. As the holder of two lucrative benefices at Utrecht and Aachen, and a professorship at Cologne, he found himself in his early thirties, like Tolstoy in his middle fifties, with a Midas-like power that turned all that he touched into a personal triumph, and yet all this glory was accompanied by a sickening sense that he had missed the substance for the shadow.

A legend says that an unknown man touched Groote on the shoulder while he was attending some athletic games in Cologne and asked, "Why standest thou here, thou oughtest to become another man," after which he disappeared in the crowd, and his name remains unknown. Soon afterward Groote was stricken with a serious illness, and in the depths of it he resolved to change his style of life and to yield himself to God, but recovering strength, he neglected the vow.

A close friendship with Hendrik van Kalkar, the prior of a Carthusian monastery at Munnikhuizen, however, led some months later to his following the course of his earlier resolve and in 1374 he gave up his two rich benefices, gave away much of his money, and encouraged a group of women who wanted to live a more intense spiritual life to use all but two rooms of his house at Deventer. Groote prepared a very free rule for them as Sisters of the Common Life.

Between 1374 and 1376, it is believed that he more than once visited the Flemish mystic Ruysbroeck in his forest cloister at Groenendael near Brussels, and that it was Ruysbroeck who counseled him to enter the Carthusian monastery of his friend Hendrik van Kalkar in order to submit his life for a period to their severe discipline. This he did from 1376 to 1379, but instead of joining this contemplative order, they agreed that his gifts of popular persuasion could be better used to preach a new devotion to his own Dutch countrymen. So, as Thomas More was to do a century and a half later, after his period of Carthusian training, he re-entered the world. Feeling unworthy to take more than a deacon's ordination, he was given a special license to preach and for the next four years, from 1379 to 1383, he moved the people of Holland as no preacher has done in their history to repent and to give themselves with a new devotion to Christ and pattern their life on His.

His free exposure of the vices of the established clergy and of the mendicant orders, and his longing for an inner reformation of the church finally resulted in their having him suppressed by getting the Bishop of Utrecht to revoke his license to preach. This action silenced Gerhard Groote at the very height of his influence for good as a preacher. With this burning message to give, Groote retired to his rooms at Deventer and in the remaining year of his brief life he gave himself to writing and to the ordering of the

Brethren of the Common Life. These Brethren were a group of men who had resolved, as the result of Groote's preaching, to give themselves to a more complete life of abandonment to God, but on a freer basis than the existing monastic orders provided. In Deventer the group lived in the vicarage of Groote's disciple, Florentius Radewin, and earned their living largely by copying manuscripts. The movement rapidly spread to other Dutch cities and all through the lower district of the Rhine. The Brethren were free to leave the group when they liked, and a number of them remained in their own homes but gave themselves more completely to works of charity, and to prayer.

Gerhard Groote saw a great need for a better educated Dutch clergy and laity, and the Brethren of the Common Life almost from the beginning took in poor boys from the country into their homes and brotherhouses and gave them board and lodging and spiritual instruction while sending them to the cathedral schools. This new devotion did not fear learning that was grounded in a deep spiritual life, and it is no accident that gradually as they became more and more devoted to education, they were drawn to set up their own schools and that they became the greatest educators in northern Europe in the fifteenth century. Nicholas of Cusa, the renowned mystic, philosopher, humanist, and ecumenical reformer of the fifteenth century; Erasmus; and Alexander Hegius the classicist, are all believed to have been educated in their schools. In 1384, a little over a year after the Bishop's order had silenced Groote, a plague broke out and Groote went to give medical aid to one of the Brethren and himself became infected and died when he was just forty-four years of age.

The attacks of the regular monastic orders on the free houses of the Brethren of the Common Life were so sharp that it seemed wise for some of the brothers who were ready for the more complete monastic vows to take on the fairly moderate vows of the Augustinian rule, and from within the monastic orders to give a protecting hand to the widespread net of lay brotherhouses. This was done, and it was in such an Augustinian house, before 1416, that Thomas a Kempis, a fully professed monk, is believed to have put together and copied out the first books of the *Imitation* which he finally arranged and presented in complete and fully-ordered form in 1441, and signed them as a copyist might well have done: "Finished and completed in the year of our Lord 1441 by the hand of brother Thomas von Kempen at Mt. St. Agnes near Zwolle." Rufus M. Jones points out that he wrote almost the same concluding note when he finished copying the Darmstadt Bible.

Who, Then, Wrote the Imitation?

Two Catholic scholars, James von Ginnekin, S.J. and Joseph Malaise, S.J., have within the last decade and a half helped to swing the theory of the authorship of the *Imitation* back to Gerhard Groote by publishing a translation from the old Netherlandish texts of the *Spiritual Diary of Gerhard Groote* which with a very few changes of order and missing chapters coincides with the a Kempis *Imitation*. They give a very convincing and plausible account of the diary having been written at different periods after Groote's conversion. This is especially impressive in the case of the last half of the third book of the *Imitation,* on "Interior Consolations," which bears very open marks of having been written by someone who had recently suffered great outward humiliation and probably by Groote in the period when he had been suddenly cut off for good from his outward vocation of preaching and compelled to see his every instinctive expectation thwarted by the Bishop's cancellation of his license to preach.

These recent findings assert that it was Groote, the

founder of the *Devotio Moderna,* and not the mild, cloister-cropped a Kempis, who is really responsible for the *Imitation,* although almost no one now casts doubt on a Kempis' editorship. Here the matter stands at the moment, but it is to be doubted if historical scholarship will ever rest content with a final solution to so perfect a scholar's problem as the authorship of the *Imitation.*

The Imitation *and the Ascetic Temper*

I have not forgotten my early resentment of the moderately ascetic tone of the *Imitation,* of what I took to be its life-denial, its contempt for the physical world, the world of the body, and what on the surface may look like its over-concern with the salvation of my own soul. But as the years have gone on, this resentment has diminished. For I have found increasing help from the *Imitation*'s restoration of perspective, its return to first principles, its querying of the significance of the beautifully-varnished prizes which secular life and learning so largely spend themselves in attaining, and its continual invitation to the reader to have done with half measures and lukewarm devotions to Christ in favor of "giving all for all."

In reading such a book, however, one must expect that it will be athwart our Western presuppositions in almost every verse. To those who regard sharp self-discipline, asceticism, mortification or monasticism as descriptions of morbid states which a healthy Christian of our generation has happily outgrown, there will be much to overcome. For this book while an implement of the New Devotion and written for the use of those in homes and in the lay brother-houses and the lay sisterhouses, as well as those in the cloisters, yet presumes that its readers are longing to live an intentionally Christian life, and it devotes itself to the intense cultivation of that life.

The temper of American Christianity is still almost untouched by the various versions of Continental crisis theology and does not depart far from Kenneth Kirk's characterization of the last-century English temper:

The message of the gospels—so theologians persuaded themselves—was to all intents and purposes identical with . . . a message of hard work, good fellowship, self-realization, and general kindliness; a *humanist* message in fact. The duty of the Christian was to surround himself with an aura of tact and generosity, and so to make the life of his less fortunate neighbors run more smoothly. In England so much more stress has been laid upon the Incarnation as sanctifying all the common things of life, that the cross in which they are all renounced is in danger of being forgotten.[6]

The cross, however, is not forgotten in the *Imitation*. It is placed squarely at the center of the life of the practicing Christian and the validity of asceticism, i.e., the giving up of some things that are admittedly good in themselves for the sake of calling our lives back to that which is best of all, is taken for granted throughout the *Imitation*. Sprinkled through the tissue of "inspired quotations" (and there are well over a thousand quotations from the Bible in the *Imitation of Christ*) are the hard sayings of Jesus that call for totality of abandonment to him:

Whoever doth not bear his own cross and come after me cannot be my disciple. . . . Whoever he be of you that renounceth not all that he hath, he cannot be my disciple. . . . Leave the dead to bury their own dead, but go thou and publish abroad the kingdom of God. . . . No man having put his hand to the plough and looking back is fit for the kingdom of God.

An Australian said recently that American Christians seem to be more interested in the fruit than in the root of religion. I cannot help thinking of that remark as I find such general admiration of Francis of Assisi, of his beautiful

[6] Kenneth Kirk, *The Vision of God* (New York: Longman's, 1934), p. 54.

Canticle of the Sun, of his preaching to the birds, of his peacemaking, of his tenderness with all. We are right; these are good fruits indeed. But at the root of Francis' life were those very ascetic practices which as a generation we are so scornful of: fasting, silence, long vigils of prayer, drastically simplified living, severe penances, undertaken when he longed to reach the life of some recalcitrant person or to attack some stubborn situation.

When a surveyor is running lines through a tract of woods, he is usually accompanied by an axman who chops out not the whole woods but any trees and brush that interfere with the surveyor's line of vision. The *Imitation* counsels the service of a similar companion for anyone who would run the lines of his life with intentional accuracy. "If thine eye offend thee pluck it out; if thine hand offend thee cut it off. . . . For what shall it profit a man if he gain the whole world and lose his own soul."

The Imitation *and the Individual*

A second temper which characterizes the *Imitation* but which you may find puts you off in reading it, is its concern with the nurture and self-discipline of the individual soul. There is no modern social gospel to the fore in this book. But there is an establishing of a root-responsibility to God from which a genuine social concern could flower out. In an age such as ours where the social concern is so much to the fore, nothing could seem more reprehensible, defeatist, or selfishly egotistical than the third- and fourth-century movement that took some fifty thousand persons into the Lybian and Egyptian deserts to live a more austere Christian life than the lax church of the day had any interest in observing. The movement bore its own justification in its craving to be nearer to God.

Chesterton, in his *Everlasting Now*, goes further and says of such an action, "They were ascetic because asceticism was

the only possible purge of the sins of the world." Quite
incidentally it is interesting to note that it was from this
group the church drew its principal theologian in the
day of the great controversy over the person of Christ, and
quite unsolicited, it was from this group that vast quanti-
ties of grain were received by the poor of Alexandria and
other African Mediterranean cities in a time of famine.
But these were by-products—never the goal. There is no
sign in the *Imitation* of Gerhard Groote's or the Brothers
and Sisters of the Common Life's concern for education.
Yet it was out of this spiritual nurture described in the
Imitation that the concern itself and the concern to have
that education spiritually centered had sprung. To a generation who are so impatient for the fruits, a further passage
from William Sullivan on the relation of the root and the
fruit will perhaps not be superfluous:

They say that to be concerned for saving one's soul is selfish,
individualistic, anti-humanitarian, anti-social. But I am bound to
say that these liberals show themselves as unable to understand
anything profoundly human as to believe anything indisputably
divine. Because a man has to save his own soul, that does not
destroy the fact that he must live in a commonwealth of souls.
. . . When we utter the word *soul,* we do not mean an isolated
thing all alone in a private boudoir, making itself pretty for in-
spection on judgment-day. That would be absurd and the religious sense is not absurd. We mean that how I act on other souls
I shall answer for to the Lord of souls. We mean that if sympathy
is diffused, responsibility is concentrated. We mean that action,
however far it spreads comes back with its recorded page, black
or white, to the one man that sent it forth, that he must read it
to the last syllable in the Presence where there is no deceiving.
Instead of destroying the social sense, I know of nothing that
could more heavily charge its energy.[7]

[7] Sullivan, *op. cit.,* pp. 151-3.

The *Imitation* presumes throughout that the roots of religion are always in this deeply-responsible, personal relationship between the soul and God and that when that relationship grows into a life of discipleship and obedience, the social has there its staunchest support.

One further presupposition closely linked to this second one is the *Imitation*'s acceptance of the beatific vision, the entry into the presence of God, as the highest good that can come to a man in this life. This experience of being directly touched by the Love in which all other love is bottomed, surpasses any other value in worth. It is for the *Imitation* as for Augustine and Thomas Aquinas, the *ens realissimum*, the goal of life. *The Cloud of Unknowing*, a little English book of devotion of the same general period, commenting on the values of the active life as compared with the contemplative life that is pointed toward that goal of being touched by this Love, says quaintly, "Active life is both begun and ended in this life. But not so contemplative life. For it is begun in this life, and shall last without end." Thus worship and prayer, for the *Imitation*, are good in themselves. For they are an entering into the very heart of God and an engaging in that which shall neither begin nor end. And their worth is not to be measured in the fashion of our Western scale-pan calculations by the ergs of added social output which they may produce.

Abbé Bremond in a sharp passage, quoted by Kenneth Kirk, puts forcefully the thesis that if the essence of prayer is a mere practical self-exhortation to activity, it does not deserve the name of prayer.

You may learn Baedeker by heart, you may book your cabin on the next boat, register your luggage, even get half-way up the gangplank; but in no language in the world does that make you a traveller. Why all these complications . . . if you are merely going to meditate on the excellence of zeal and train yourself for

your apostolate? Have done with these whimsical exercises. Rise
from your knees. Get off at once to your desk and write your
sermon or go to the hospital and care for your patients.

Kirk continues:

Call it [prayer] a mere auxiliary to activity, and you have made
it an eccentricity with which, if you are logical, you must allow
the majority of Christians to dispense altogether. Its character has
been hopelessly compromised. It has degenerated into an epiphe-
nomenon of the moral life, a pietistic form of self-suggestion
proper only for sick souls.[8]

Therefore, when the *Imitation* says, "Blessed are those who
are glad to have time to spare for God," it means exactly
that. And it does not in modern fashion hasten to add that
if you are glad to have time to spare for God you will have
a guaranteed increase in your effectiveness in the active
tasks of life. In the *Imitation* prayer is itself an action that
needs no justification in terms of other activity, for in
prayer we fulfill the deepest yearning of our being.

I hesitate to add a further remark lest it confuse rather
than clarify what has just been expressed. Yet it has often
occurred to me that the great divide in climate between the
Imitation and the mind of our time can be swiftly exposed,
and we can know on which side of it we ourselves stand, by
asking ourselves whether or not we can justify the existence
of the contemplative orders who spend their time exclusively in prayer. When a missionary bishop says that in
reducing a province in China to an awareness of God's
presence he counts a contemplative order of ten who do
nothing but pray worth twenty active field missionaries,
does this seem rank nonsense to us? When a nineteenth
century philosopher suggests that if one man could by
prayer and self-discipline slow down the ravening desires in

[8] Kirk, *op. cit.,* p. 450.

himself, by that very act he actually would slow down and make easier the conquest of the desire life in all mankind, and hence participate from the inside in the drama of salvation, does this have any bearing on the legitimacy of the life of prayer undertaken by and for itself, but in its depths involving every creature in the universe? Søren Kierkegaard in his *Purity of Heart* puts the same problem when, in order to cleanse the issue of the modern Western accent on outward action, he chooses as his character the Incurable Sufferer who cannot possibly benefit himself in this world; who cannot cure his disease, lengthen his life, improve his action for he can no longer act. Does the self-abandonment to God in prayer of this Incurable Sufferer really matter? Does he have an apostolate of prayer in and out of his suffering?

I realize that these questions point beyond the *Imitation,* but they point beyond it in a direction that was the climate of that time, and that the reading of the *Imitation,* if we can overcome our repulsion, may point us back into: a climate where one writes not *work and contemplation,* but *contemplation and work,* or even *contemplation as work—* work which when it is the contemplation of the God revealed in Jesus Christ, draws us nearer to our fellow's work as the ego-disinfecting ground of the truest charity, and works in advancing that nearness to, and responsibility for, our fellows as no other activity in all creation can do. Yet according to the temper of the *Imitation* it is work undertaken of and for itself, since to know God is the most excellent of all things.

The Psychology of the Imitation

This introduction has been long. It must now give way to a brief look into the *Imitation* itself. The style seems to have been shaped by the Bible. Much of it is Wisdom

Literature with sharp epigrammatic Confucian-like state-
ments that compress within a line or two what a volume of
commentary could not improve upon. But there are long
passages that read like prayers of contrition and aspiration,
and recall the Psalms.

If, as seems plausible, this book is the spiritual diary of
Gerhard Groote, it shows the mellowing and tendering of a
stiff, stubborn Dutch will as the background for the re-
peated cycles of admonitions that the heart must ever speak
to itself. But whether it is Groote's book or not, the *Imitation* is a campaigner's manual with minute instructions for
turning a raw, unripe recruit who is full of romantic enthusiasm for following Jesus, into a seasoned veteran who
has more and more exchanged the insatiable slavery of his
ego-centered life for the spacious liberty of a life lived in
quiet, steady abandon to the hidden life and will of God,
and who is now made ready to follow Christ without reser-
vation.

Ignatius of Loyola, whose *Spiritual Exercises* owe an
enormous debt to the *Imitation,* begins his thirty-day period
of retreat with days of meditation on what he calls the
Foundation, i.e., what are you here on earth for anyway?
And the *Imitation* in which he nurtured himself, suggests
"when you have read and learned many things, you must
nevertheless go back to the one principle." [9]

My son, I ought to be thy supreme and ultimate end if thou
desire to be truly blessed. For if in anything thou seekest thyself,
immediately thou faintest and driest up. I have bestowed all, and
my will is to have all of thee again. If Heavenly grace enter in
and true charity, there will be no envy nor narrowness of heart,
neither will self-love busy itself. For Divine charity overcometh
all things, and enlargeth all the powers of the soul.[10]

[9] *Imitation of Christ,* III, 43.
[10] *Ibid.,* III, 9.

This is the foundation, the first principle of life which a sound grasp of order leads the *Imitation* to lay down. It is because our souls are made in such a way that only as they come aware of their ground in God and, casting themselves upon it, as they seek to live from it rather than from the frantic ego, "all of the powers of the soul are enlarged." The *Imitation*'s psychology is contained in this. For it, then, the fully normal man is the man who has not only learned this truth but who knows it inwardly. Such a normal man is described in the line, "in the fervent spiritual man there is true peace," and "inward liberty."

"The Pulses of the Divine Whisper"

The *Imitation* gives glimpses here and there of the swift, direct, firsthand inward experiences that "inflame within" and light up the inward course of life as flashes of lightning on a dark night illumine the whole countryside and give us our bearings so that we may go on even when we do not see.

Enlarge Thou me in love, that with the inward palate of my heart I may taste how sweet it is to love and to be dissolved and as it were to bathe myself in Thy love. . . .[11] Blessed is he to whom Truth manifests itself not by figures and passing words, but such as It is in itself. . . .[12] Blessed is the soul which heareth the Lord speaking within her, and receiveth from His mouth the word of consolation. Blessed are the ears that gladly receive the pulses of the divine whisper . . . which listen not after the voice which is sounding without but for the Truth teaching inwardly. . . . [13] Let all doctors hold their peace, let all creatures keep silent in thy sight, speak Thou alone to me.[14]

[11] *Ibid.*, III, 6.
[12] *Ibid.*, I, 3.
[13] *Ibid.*, III, 1.
[14] *Ibid.*, II, 3.

In the reading of Scripture, which the *Imitation* in the full flow of the New Devotion strongly recommends, the reader is bidden to wait upon the direct inward illumination. Of the prophets it says:

Most beautifully do they speak, but if Thou be silent, they inflame not the heart. What they can do is only without, but Thou instructest and enlightenest the heart. They water outwardly, but Thou givest fruitfulness. They cry aloud in words, but Thou impartest understanding to the hearing. Let not Moses, therefore, speak unto me, but Thou, Lord my God, the Everlasting Truth; lest I die and prove unfaithful if I be only warned outwardly and not inflowed within.[15]

The *Imitation* also quotes Eckhart almost word for word in one of his most audacious declarations that if man would but make a void God must flow in, when it puts into God's address: "If you could wholly annihilate yourself and free yourself fully from the love of creatures, then would I flow into you with great graces." [16] And again, "I would gladly speak to you my word and manifest to you my secrets, if you would only diligently watch for my coming and open unto Me the door of your heart." [17]

Of the morally purifying and settling effect of such inward inflammation, the *Imitation* has two strong lines: "An iron put into the fire loses its rust and becomes clearly red hot so that he who wholly turneth himself unto God puts off all slothfulness and is transformed into a new man." [18] and: "He in whom the Eternal Word speaks is delivered from many opinions."

Yet like all mature counselors on these kindling flashes that are given now and then for the encouragement of the

[15] *Ibid.*, III, 2.
[16] *Ibid.*, III, 42.
[17] *Ibid.*, III, 24.
[18] *Ibid.*, II, 4.

pilgrim, they are not to be confused with the abandonment itself, and the *Imitation*'s words are stern as they warn: "And reckon it not a great thing nor imagine God loves you especially when you feel great devotion and sweetness; for it is not by this that a true lover of virtues is recognized, nor is it in this that the progress and perfection of man consists." [19]

There are three verses in the twentieth chapter of the first book of the *Imitation* that might suitably be used to focus this encouragement of mature abandonment to Christ which it is the purpose of the manual to further: "No man doth safely speak, but he that is willing to hold his peace. No man doth safely appear abroad, but he who can gladly abide at home, out of sight. No man can safely command others but he that hath learned willingly to obey."

"No Man Doth Safely Speak"

The *Imitation* is full of strong testimony to the necessity of the conquest of the tongue, and to the tendering power of silent prayer. The ceaseless idle talk in which as under a compulsive obsession most people spend their time, the *Imitation* counsels the recruit for abandonment to God to shun.

Avoid the concourse of people as much as possible, for to hear much of what happens here and there becomes a great hindrance, even though it be told with the purest intention. For we are easily defiled and enslaved by vanity. But why is it that we are so fond of talking and chatting with one another when we so seldom return to our solitude without a wounded conscience? The reason why we are so fond of talking is that we look for consolation by conversing with others. And we prefer to talk of those things to which we are inclined and which are most to our liking or also of those things which we most dislike. But alas it

[19] *Ibid.,* III, 26.

is often-times to no purpose. For this outward consolation is no small hindrance to interior and divine consolation. . . .[20] It is no small prudence to keep silence in an evil time and inwardly to turn thyself to Me and not be troubled by the judgments of men.[21]

It is this compulsive obsession to speak that the *Imitation* would pare away, in order to cultivate in man and woman the true art of interior listening for the pulses of the divine whisper. To be able to sit in a company, if it is necessary to be in company, and to let others say what you would have said and be glad that you were relieved of the burden of saying it, to listen and to attend inwardly, to be able to speak or not to speak—not according to the compulsive obsession of garrulity, or of a desire to be admired or to air some private grievance, but rather according to whether something helpful will not be contributed if you remain silent is to cut away the egotism of the tongue and restore the level of true communication. "No man doth safely speak, but he who is willing to hold his peace." "When it is permissible to talk," continues the *Imitation*, "speak of things that are profitable and edifying. It is no small help to our spiritual progress when we speak together of spiritual things, especially with those who have one heart and one soul with us in God." [22]

The power of specific acts of silent recollection is often recommended in the *Imitation*.

If thou canst not continually recollect thyself, yet do it sometimes, at least once a day, namely in the morning or at night. In the morning fix thy good purpose; and at night examine thyself, what thou hast done, how thou hast behaved in word, deed

---

[20] *Ibid.*, I, 20.
[21] *Ibid.*, III, 28.
[22] *Ibid.*, I, 20.

and thought. . . .[23] If thou desirest true contrition of heart, enter into thy secret chamber and shut out the tumults of the world. . . . In silence and in stillness, a religious soul advantageth herself, and learneth the mysteries of Holy Scripture. Shut thy door upon thee, and call upon Jesus thy Beloved. Stay with him in thy closet; for thou shalt not find so great peace anywhere else.[24]

"No Man Doth Safely Appear Abroad"

The *Imitation*, with a psychological wisdom born of deep self-knowledge, puts its finger here on another symptom of ego-centered slavery: the manic flight from the true self into activity, change of scene, change of intimates, change of job, movement from place to place:

The imagination and the desire for change of residence have deceived many a one. . . .[25] They who wander much abroad seldom thereby become holy.[26] The place availeth little if the spirit of fervor be wanting, neither shall that place long continue, which is sought from without. Thou mayest change but not better thyself. For when occasion arises and is laid hold of, thou shalt find what thou dost flee from and more too.[27]

As the old Dutch housewife in Edna Ferber's *So Big* tells the young woman teacher, "You can't run away from life, Missy, you can't run away far enough." The *Imitation* with its characteristic maturity knows too well how readily the ego may seek to throw the Hound of Heaven off the scent in order to elude the pain of its committal to the way of abandonment by storming a man with a restless impulse to leave the room, to gad about, to do something, anything, else; to go somewhere, anywhere, else; rather than to face

[23] *Ibid.*, I, 19.
[24] *Ibid.*, I, 20.
[25] *Ibid.*, I, 9.
[26] *Ibid.*, I, 23.
[27] *Ibid.*, III, 27.

the first principle of his life within the four walls of this very room, within this difficult family situation, or within this congregation, and let his life be ordered by it. Donne Byrne once wrote, "The hardest battle of my life was fought within the walls of this little room"; and among the wise maxims of the Desert Fathers is the figure: "Even as a tree cannot bear fruit if it be often transplanted, no more can a monk that is always moving from one place to another." [28] There is no attempt in the *Imitation* to compare one position with another, as if we were to glorify the great Protestant pastor-saint of the Vosges, Jean Frédéric Oberlin, who in a forty-year pastorate transformed a region and said, "ten years to make a diagnosis, ten years to carry it out, ten years to correct and improve it," and were then to jeer at the minister who changed his church so often that his old hens, when he came home from conference, lay on their backs and stuck up their feet to be tied. It is not staying versus leaving. The *Imitation* goes deeper. To the raw recruit it says, distrust this restless passion for change of place. Immobilize yourself, stay put in your room, until the restless ego has been crucified in you and the abandonment has proceeded to the point where you are willing either to stay at home or to go abroad, either to keep your present post or to move to another. When you are beyond the compulsive flight from yourself and from God, then and only then can you avail yourself of the broad freedom of responding to His will either by remaining or going out as He commands.

"No Man Can Safely Command Others"

The *Imitation* is not an officer's manual and is certainly as little interested in teaching men how to command or

[28] Helen Waddell, *The Desert Fathers* (New York: Sheed & Ward, 1936) , p. 126.

rule over their fellows as a book could be. Yet, it would point out that only those who are under the command of God, and who are broken inwardly in their own pride, are fit to assist others in the process of breaking their self-will. Jesus asks the soul: "How can you be Mine and I be yours, unless you be detached both inwardly and outwardly from self-will." [29]

To learn to obey is to learn to yield one's own will, to look on calmly and see his own pride wither away, to yield his own fierce passion for self-sufficiency. It is hard to believe that it is anyone other than Gerhard Groote writing a chapter from his own experience in suffering the silencing of his mission to preach, when the *Imitation* says: "There is scarcely anything wherein it is harder to mortify yourself than in seeing and suffering things against your will; especially when you are commanded something which seems unreasonable and useless." [30] The *Imitation*, however, is not content alone to explain what the terrifying monastic vow of obedience to a superior is meant to do in literally breaking the surface will in order to assist the deeper abandonment to God. It gives many illustrations of occasions, in the daily life of one living in any society, that lay a cross upon the will and that can be used to open us to our true end.

The *Imitation* suggests that one of the surest ways to find whether self-will and pride in self still reigns in us is to hear ourselves spoken against or criticized:

Words after all are only words.
They fly through the air, but they hurt not a stone.
If you are guilty, think that you would gladly amend yourself; and if you are conscious of your innocence, consider that you would gladly suffer this for the love of God.

[29] *Imitation of Christ*, III, 37.
[30] *Ibid.*, III, 49.

It is little enough that now and then you should suffer a few
words, you who are as yet unable to stand heavy blows.

Why do you take to heart such trivial things, except that you are
still too carnal and have too much human respect.

For you are afraid to be despised; you are unwilling to be blamed
for your defects; and you always seek to exculpate yourself. Now
look into yourself more carefully and you will find out that the
world lives in you, as well as the vain desire to please men.

If you are unwilling to be humiliated and put to shame for your
defects it is evident that you are not yet truly humble nor truly
dead to the world, and that the world is not yet crucified in you.

But listen to My word and you will not care for even two thousand words of men.

If all the evil which can be maliciously invented, were spoken
against you, what harm could it do you if you ignored it and
considered it were chaff?

Can all this talk remove a hair from your head? [31]

And then come two matchless verses that gather up these
admonitions on the way to bear words that criticize us: "He
whose heart is not recollected within, and has not God
before his eyes, becomes easily disturbed by a word of re-
proach. Whereas he who trusts in Me, and does not justify
himself in his own eyes, will be free from the fear of men.
For I am the Judge: I know all the secrets." [32]

So long as this life goes on one must remain vulnerable
to such attack, although a later chapter remarks, "Sometimes you will be given a consolation, but never to full
satisfaction." [33] A friend of mine who is the president of a
prominent Negro college and who was for years under fire
both from within and from without by detractors who
accused him, now of reaction, and now of revolutionary

[31] *Ibid.*, III, 41.
[32] *Ibid.*, III, 46.
[33] *Ibid.*, III, 49.

intentions, told me of a consoling visit he received one day
when the detraction was at its sharpest. An old Negro
preacher called at his office and asked his secretary if he
could see the president. She inquired, and the man was
admitted. He came up to my friend, took his hand, and told
him: "Mr. President, I've been hearing what they've been
saying about you, and I won't keep you long. I'm a great
student of trees, Mr. President. I've been studying them all
my life, and I just wanted to tell you that when I see a tree
with the bark all skinned off the trunk and with sticks and
stones and brickbats lying under it, I don't need to look up
any further, I know for certain it's a fruit tree. Good morning, Mr. President, God bless you." And he hobbled out.
The attacks continued for several years and have never entirely died out. "Sometimes you will be given a consolation,
but never to full satisfaction."

The consolations, however, according to the *Imitation,*
are less valuable in stripping us of self-will than the humiliations, and as for those who come to us to rebuke our faults,
they are great benefactors if we can but learn to agree with
them and to receive them gratefully. "It is often very profitable to keep us more humble, that others know and rebuke
our faults. When a man humbleth himself for his failings,
then he easily pacifieth others and quickly satisfieth those
that are offended with him." [34]

Of the daily mortifications that help develop abandonment to God and willing obedience to Him, the catalogue
in the forty-ninth chapter of the third book of the *Imitation* is discerning:

You must often do the things you do not like; and the things
you do like you must leave undone. What pleases others will suc-
ceed; what pleases you will be a failure. What others say will be

[34] *Ibid.,* III, 2.

listened to; but what you say will be accounted as nothing. Others ask and receive; you ask and remain unheard. Others are praised by men; you are passed over in silence. Others are assigned to one position or another; but you are accounted fit for nothing. Although you bear it in silence your nature will sometimes grieve at this and cause no small struggle within you. In these and many other things, the faithful servant of God is tested how far he can renounce himself and break his own will in all things.[35]

In the bearing of these crosses the emphasis in the *Imitation* is always upon the principle of learning obedience to God, learning abandonment to Him as our tough gristly self-will is pared away.

It is good for us that we sometimes suffer contradictions and that we are misjudged even when we do what is right. Such humiliations may shield us from vainglory. For when a man of good will is downtrodden and outwardly despised and discredited or when he is tormented with evil intentions within, then he realizes that he has greater need of God without whom he can do nothing.[36]

It is in the spirit of the verse, "My son be not disturbed when you see others advanced and honored and yourself despised and humiliated," [37] that George Herbert can comment on his having been passed over and another man appointed to a high church post:

> How know I if Thou shouldst me raise
> That I should thus raise Thee
> Perhaps great places and Thy praise
> Do not so well agree.

Thus all crosses in this life that make us malleable, that open in us the fountain of tears, and give us the molten heart, that plow and harrow and drag and disk the tough

[35] *Ibid.*, III, 49.
[36] *Ibid.*, I, 12.
[37] *Ibid.*, III, 41.

root-clogged surface-will of our lives until it is a mellow
seedbed for the Seed—these things alone make any man fit,
if he can ever be declared to be fit, to guide and to direct
others. "No man can safely command others, but he that
hath learned willingly to obey."

But the *Imitation* does not simply prescribe ascetic exercises for the softening of the sclerotic will. It presents no
empty cross of negation. On its cross a man hangs, a man
whose company all may count upon in extremity. Central
throughout the *Imitation* is this figure of Jesus Christ.
There is in the Christ of the *Imitation* little that depicts
the Jesus at the wedding feast, with his friends at Bethany,
with little children, or healing the sick. It is rather Jesus
Christ the suffering servant of the fifty-third chapter of
Isaiah, Jesus Christ of the Passion week that is most prominent. Perhaps the best known chapter in the *Imitation*
is called "The Royal Road of the Holy Cross," where we
are invited to "suffer with Christ if thou desire to reign
with Christ" and are warned that "there is no other way
unto life and into true inward peace but the way of the
Holy Cross and of daily mortification." [38]

The plea "to conform the life wholly to the life of Christ"
as the goal of this life is central, however, and in a fourth
section is supplemented by the strong encouragement of the
reader in this process of life conformity by the regular par-
ticipation in the sacramental life of the church.

It is always the *life* of the aspirant and never his learning
or his outward appearance that is put to the fore. Here the
New Devotion's reform of life is prominent. The egotism
of the intellect is seldom more pleasantly scoffed at than in
such lines as, "My son it behoves you to be ignorant of many
things." [39] "When the day of judgment comes, we shall not
be asked how much we have read but what we have done,

[38] *Ibid.*, II, 12.
[39] *Ibid.*, III, 44.

not how well we have spoken, but how well we have lived." [40] "I am He who in a single moment can so enlighten the heart of man that he will know more than if he had studied ten years in the schools." [41]

The Homely Wisdom of the Imitation

Throughout the *Imitation* there is a tone of realistic moderation that reassures the reader who may have wondered at times what manner of holy men lived in Holland in the fourteenth and fifteenth centuries. That they were frail flesh-and-blood men, never out of the reach of temptation so long as they drew breath is made abundantly plain throughout the *Imitation*. "Be more patient of soul," the *Imitation* urges, "Thou art a man, and not God; thou art flesh, not an angel." [42] "But *never* to feel disturbance nor any weariness of mind or body; that does not pertain to this life, but to the state of eternal rest." [43] There is no desire to crush out life but rather only to order it.

Behold meat, drink, clothes and other necessaries for the maintenance of the body are burdensome unto a fervent spirit. Grant me to use such refreshments moderately and not be entangled with an over-great desire of them. It is not lawful to cast away all things because nature is to be sustained, but to acquire superfluities, the holy law forbiddeth us.[44]

And then follows a line worthy of engraving on the tablets of the heart, "Do not have that which may entangle and deprive thee of inward liberty." [45]

[40] *Ibid.*, I, 3.
[41] *Ibid.*, III, 44.
[42] *Ibid.*, III, 57.
[43] *Ibid.*, II, 20.
[44] *Ibid.*, III, 26.
[45] *Ibid.*, III, 27.

Père Jean Grou, who although a French contemporary of Lafayette, is, thanks to von Hügel, well known to our time, has given a mature account of devotion when he declares that it "is not a thing that passes, which comes and goes as it were, but it is something habitual, fixed, permanent which extends over every instant of life, and regulates all our conduct" and it is to this mature devotion to Christ that the *Imitation* would lead us.

Jesus Christ says, My son, trust not your affections which easily change from one thing to another. As long as you live you will be changeful in spite of yourself, so that you will find yourself joyful at one time and sad at another; now peaceful, now disturbed; now devout and diligent, now slothful; now heavy now light of heart. But a wise man, well experienced in the spiritual life, is superior to these vicissitudes; he pays no attention to what he feels within himself nor from what direction the wind of inconstancy blows; but he cares only to direct the intentions of his heart to the right end. For thus he may remain unmoved and undisturbed, if through all these various events he directs the simple eye of his intention continually toward Me. The purer the interior eye is, the steadier one passes through the storm.[46]

The closing line may well conclude this little engagement with the *Imitation*, for to a generation which will have to ride a storm whose beginning alone is as yet visible, the *Imitation* is a storm almanac that is worthy of being kept open beside us as we stand watch on the bridge.

[46] *Ibid.*, III, 34.

2

Francis de Sales and the
Introduction to the Devout Life

CHAPTER 2

Francis de Sales and the
Introduction to the Devout Life

FROM the stern forbidding Dutch *Imitation of Christ*
to the gay inviting French-Italian *Introduction to the
Devout Life* there is not only the geographical separation
of Holland and Savoy, nor the gap of two religiously tu-
multuous centuries, but there is also the span of two temperaments that couch the same truths in radically different form. To the French mind, Francis de Sales, the
author of the *Introduction* was always a provincial, an up-
lander, a native of the High Savoy who spent his life in
service to the mountain people of this northern tip of the
curious corridor kingdom that connected France and Italy.
And yet the deft French touch that characterized all that
he did and wrote made them look upon him as one of the
first rank of their own, and the fact that they could not
dislodge him from Savoy and that he steadfastly refused
both royal favor and high clerical office in France may
even have heightened this regard of theirs.

The story of Francis de Sales' own life can be swiftly
told. He was born in 1567 near Annecy, a provincial capital
in the High Savoy some fifty miles southwest of Geneva. He
was the eldest son of a devout Catholic family who belonged

to the nobility. He was given the best education the time could afford, with seven years in Savoy, seven university years at Paris and then three taking a doctorate in canon and civil law at Padua, a total of seventeen years of hard study. At the age of twenty-four he was highly honored by his doctoral examiners at Padua. He returned to Savoy and with high civil employment at his disposal, he entered the church and after serving only a year as provost of the cathedral at Annecy, he turned his back on all the secure roads to preferment and volunteered to go on a dangerous mission task in the Chablais along the southern shores of Lake Geneva. The stout Calvinistic Protestants in this district not only sought to out-debate any rivals but thought nothing of ambushing Catholic mission priests, and his father despaired of his life. He spent four years directing the mission work in this region and had a number of almost miraculous escapes. His gentle approach that insisted that the way to win heretics was to preach the love and not the fear of God, accomplished more than any of his predecessors had been able to do. He was recalled to Annecy in 1598 as bishop coadjutor and became "Bishop of Geneva" in 1602, a post which he faithfully served for twenty years until his death in 1622.

It was in this closing twenty years that he emerged as a mission preacher and as a director of souls that had few peers in all of France. Whether it was a person of the highest rank or whether it was a deaf and dumb servant in his own household, he gave himself without reserve to his needs. His correspondence was enormous, amounting to from fifteen to twenty carefully written letters a day year in and year out throughout this period. Winter and summer he rose at four in the morning, gave himself to prayer and then to his day's work. He wrote his own letters employing no secretary. He believed his correspondents would feel freer if they knew that all was under four eyes and four alone. A small portion of these letters fill eleven volumes of his published works. While preaching a Lenten series of sermons in Lyon in 1604, he touched the life of Madame Jane Chantal who soon looked to him for spiritual guidance. In 1610, after her widowhood, she came to Annecy and Francis founded for her the important women's contemplative Order of the Visitation which he guided with minute care for the remaining years of his life.

There is a good deal of evidence to indicate that Francis de Sales' own spiritual development was greatly aided by his close association with the great mystic Jane Chantal in the last twenty years of his life and that the cautious advice of the *Introduction to the Devout Life* is as far surpassed in the intimate firsthand account of the mystical life in the *Treatise on the Love of God* as William Law's *Serious Call to the Devout Life* is capped by his later writings on *Prayer* after Law had come under the influence of the mystic Jacob Boehme. I have carefully reread both the *Introduction* and the *Treatise* within the last months, and I believe such a contrast to be true, but to be an exaggerated truth. For there is nothing in the *Introduction to the Devout Life* that I find taken back in the *Treatise*. The *Treatise* only extends and deepens the sound lines that were already there in the *Introduction* just as Francis' own life of prayer was extended and deepened but in the same direction by this wonderful association with Jane Chantal and the Order of the Visitation which he founded for her.

It was for the encouragement of the newly founded Order of the Visitation that he prepared his *Treatise on the Love of God*, perhaps the most readable and usable book still in existence in that border field between ascetic and mystical theology. The substance of this great book he gave to these nuns as he was preparing it, and their memories of these informal talks given to half a dozen of them in their little gallery house at Annecy, or out under the grape arbor near their orchard, were set down by them and later published as his *Spiritual Conferences.*

How the Introduction *Was Written*

The famous *Introduction to the Devout Life* was first published in 1609 and achieved an immediate success. There is no dispute about its authorship, but the circumstances surrounding its origin have been a good deal discussed. Was it, or was it not simply a set of letters written to Madame Charmoisy for her spiritual guidance?

The most plausible account would seem to be that Francis de Sales, a distant relative and close friend of Claude de Charmoisy, had known the wife, Madame Louise Charmoisy, from the time of their marriage in 1600, but early in 1607 in Annecy she heard a sermon by Francis that kindled in her a desire to give herself more completely to God. She sought his help as a spiritual guide, drew up a set of resolutions, saw him often, and it was after this period that their frequent correspondence began. He wrote of Madame Charmoisy to Jane Chantal in April 1607, "I have just found in our sacred nets a fish which I had so longed for these four years. It is a lady all gold, and magnificently fitted to serve her Saviour; and if she persevere she will do so with fruit."

In the exchange of correspondence with Madame Charmoisy, Francis apparently sent to her certain papers containing directions for use in her own spiritual development which he had prepared from time to time as others had requested similar help during the preceding five years. The systematic Madame Charmoisy had also carefully set down the oral counsel which Francis had given her and had organized all of these directions according to their subjects.

Early the next year, she had occasion to show them to Father Fourier, the director of the Jesuit College in Chambery, where she was staying, and Fourier, who had earlier been Francis de Sales' own spiritual director, was so impressed with them that he wrote to Francis and asked him to prepare these papers promptly for publication in order that many could profit by them.

Speaking of Father Fourier's reaction to these notes, Madame Charmoisy wrote to Francis, "he found them so beautiful that he assured me he had never read anything more useful or more edifying; this is also the feeling of all the Fathers of the College to whom he showed them. They took copies and are resolved to publish the book if you do not do it yourself." Francis replied, "It is a singular thing that according to these good Fathers I have composed a book without having the slightest intention of doing so." [1]

Henry IV, who had apparently also heard the rumor of the existence of this manuscript, had directed M. Deshazes to write to Francis urging him to issue a book

in which religion should be shown in all its native beauty, stripped of all superstition and scruple, practical for all classes of society, at court, in camp, compatible with the agitations of the world and the bustle of business—equally opposed to the laxity which flatters sinners and the severity which discourages them. Such a book was wanting and no one [declared the King] was better able to write it than the Bishop of Geneva.[2]

Francis took back this material from Madame Charmoisy and addressing it to a lover of God, "Philothea" who is to remain in the thick of secular life but who yet would offer her life to God in that station, he completed in a few

[1] M. M. Maxwell-Scott, *St. Francis de Sales and His Friends* (St. Louis: B. Herder, 1913), p. 195.
[2] *Ibid.*, p. 196.

months the manuscript of the *Introduction to the Devout Life* which was published in Lyons early in 1609. The book was thoroughly revised and worked over and added to in three further editions, and the present volume is a translation of the fourth and final edition which appeared in 1619, three years before Francis' death.

The Guidance of Souls

Whether Madame Charmoisy was the exclusive object of the spiritual directions set down in the *Introduction* or, as it seems more probable, whether she was not, does not, however, in any way alter a more important fact. Whoever they were written for, these directions came from the hand of a deeply spiritual and highly skilled director of souls whose method is important for us to understand today.

It is true that the title "director of souls" has an alien sound to a Free Churchman's ears. Many in our time would scoff at it and insist that they wanted no human being to meddle with their souls or their relations to God. Yet it is equally true that many within the Free Churches and many on the borders of their ranks who would hardly acknowledge a formal religious affiliation are wistful and looking expectantly now to the psychotherapists both sacred and secular, now to some free fellowship group, or now to some religious prophet in the hope that their spiritually immature lives or their initial revulsion from their obsession with self may find some nurture.

It is not for them a question of initial evangelism. Life has convinced them that there is a deeper way. But what shall they do next? It is to these very people that Francis de Sales speaks in his *Introduction*. He offers his services as a seasoned director, as one who knows God and devotion to Him at first hand, but who also knows, both from himself and from others, the heights and the depths of a man, his heroism and his weakness, and speaks out of this knowledge; and it will be a proud and self-sufficient Free Churchman who on account of a title will reject this offer of help if he is in real need. Francis, however, goes further and tells those who would grow in the spiritual life to find some wise counselor and seek his advice. Francis points out in one of his conferences that Paul was converted by the direct intervention of God—but was then told to go to Ananias, "a man who will tell you what to do." God is always the first director of souls for Francis, and he is reluctant to do more than give elementary exercises leading toward detachment and prayer where each soul will find its own true course inwardly confirmed for him.

Although the *Introduction* was one of the most influential books that emerged from the sixteenth-century Catholic Renaissance which the Protestant Reformation had helped to prick into life, the actual method of spiritual guidance that it set forth contains little that is new. Ignatius has expressed the essence of it in his famous outline for a thirty-day retreat called the *Spiritual Exercises*. Theresa of Ávila has said it all before in her counsel to her nuns in the *Way of Perfection*. Scupoli has hammered grimly away at it in the *Spiritual Combat* that Francis de Sales carried as a pocket talisman in his younger years. As you read the *Introduction* you are drawn to say, "I have read all of this before," but in the same breath you are haunted by the certainty that you have never before seen it put so well, so fervently, so attractively and addressed so specifically to those who must live in the world.

Lawrence Housman once said in describing Francis of Assisi that a saint was one who made goodness attractive, and certainly by this standard the Salesian description of the life of devotion has the saintly touch. For from the opening paragraph the Salesian charm is at work recommending long-tried practices of discipline, prayer and corporate worship by a perfect façade of effective anecdote and analogy, and lighted up everywhere by a personal tenderness and understanding of man's inward needs that disarm the wary reader and tend to open him to the practice of the wise and well-ordered instructions that follow. This charm, this fervency, this restatement of sound practice in ways that open the heart to it is perhaps the first observation that should be set down about the genius of Francis de Sales' method.

Sources of the Salesian Approach

But this is not alone a genius of exposition. The *Introduction* rests on theological principles that like all great theology have come out of devotional experience. Francis had the great privilege of being both an inheritor of the Spanish Carmelite mystical experience of Theresa of Ávila and of having this inwardly confirmed in an early and absolutely determinative experience in his own life while he was a student at Paris and checked and deepened again and again in his later life as a man of prayer.

The early experience can scarcely be better told than in the following account given by Jane Chantal:

The Blessed one told me once to strengthen me in a certain trouble of my own, that as a student at Paris, he fell into great temptation and exceeding agonies of mind, being convinced in himself that he was eternally rejected without hope of salvation and this made him numb with terror . . . notwithstanding this extremity of suffering, in his heart he always preserved his resolution of loving and serving God to the best of his powers through this life, with all the more affection and loyalty since he thought he would have no further opportunity in Eternity. This torment endured within him for at least three or nearly six weeks so violently that he lost appetite and sleep and became thin and yellow as wax. But on the day appointed by Divine Providence for his deliverance, as he passed a church he turned in to kneel before a Lady-altar, where he beheld the prayer *memorare* fastened to a board. He said it through, then rising it came to him all at once that his disease had fallen from him like leperous scales, and he felt himself perfectly and completely whole.[3]

He later told his early biographer Camus that it was from this experience that he learned "to have compassion on the infirmities of others" and he once wrote a soul similarly afflicted: "My soul, which endured the like for six long weeks, is qualified to compassionate those thus afflicted." [4] His later biographer Hamon declares he heard at the crucial moment the line, "I do not call myself the Damning one, my name is Jesus."

Abbé Brémond writes of this experience: "Emotions, the most vehement pass, but principles remain. It was not the heart alone of the saint which was formed in this trial; his mind, thought, theology were likewise molded." [5] He received, in other words, not alone "a message of peace, but a doctrine of pacification."

Out of this student crisis, the mission experience in Chablais, the study of Christian doctrine, his own prayer life and his early responsibilities in the confessional and as a guide of souls, there grew in Francis a theology that was grounded in a passionate confidence in the infinite mercy and grace of God, in the divine initiative always operative upon the souls of men, and in at least a rudimentary capacity for response to His love that in this life at least is never absent from the souls of men. One has only to read the

[3] Abbé Henri Brémond, *History of Religious Thought in France* (New York: The Macmillan Company, 1928–1936), I, p. 68.

[4] *Ibid.*, p. 68.

[5] *Ibid.*, p. 69.

first book of the *Treatise on the Love of God* to see that
here is no denial of original sin or of the need of God's
mercy and grace. Yet Francis insists that there remains in
man a fragment of the original discerning power so that
"as soon as a man thinks with even a little attention of the
divinity, he feels a certain delightful motion of the heart
which testifies that God is God of the human heart." [6]

This natural inclination then which we have to love God above
all things is not left for nothing in our hearts: for on God's
part it is a handle by which he can hold us and draw us to himself;—and the divine goodness seems in some sort by this impression to keep our hearts tied as little birds in a string by
which he can draw us when it pleases his mercy to take pity
upon us—and on our part it is a mark and memorial of our
first principal and creator, to whose love it moves us, giving us
a secret intimation that we belong to his divine goodness; even
as harts upon whom princes have had collars put with their
coats of arms, though afterwards they cause them to be let loose
and run at liberty in the forest, do not fail to be recognized by
anyone who meets them not only as having been once taken by
the prince whose arms they bear, but also as being still reserved
for him. [7]

Salesian Gentleness

It is always to man as a wearer of the Prince's collar no
matter how deeply concealed it may be that Francis speaks
in his direction of souls, and this is the pivot of what looks
on the surface as being his mild and benign method of
dealing with the nurture of souls. For he knew and continually relied on God's prior and subsequent action upon
the soul and upon the soul's capacity to respond to that
action. He knew too well that unless that response of the

[6] *Treatise on the Love of God*, p. 54.
[7] *Ibid.*, p. 62.

soul itself took over, no change of life would be lasting. Bullying of souls too often reveals a failure to acknowledge this prior action of God's grace and a failure to acknowledge the soul's own inherent capacity to respond to that love, and Francis scrupulously refrained from it. Merciless as he was with himself, he was very gentle with others. "He who wins the heart, wins all" was always his motto. Francis expresses this with great clarity when he declares:

We must not evince an absolute and dominating spirit: the human will is not forced. You must gain it by gentle persuasion. You must knock gently at the door of men's hearts, you must gently force them to open. If you are successful you effect a happy cure: if you are rejected, then with gentleness must your rejection be received. In the royal galley of divine love there is no convict labor: all the oarsmen are volunteers. God endures resistance to his inspirations and does not cease those inspirations on that account in spite of rejection of his call.[8]

In 1602 he wrote to some nuns in Paris:

I suspect myself that there is another hindrance to your reform. Possibly those who have proposed it to you have handled the wound over-harshly. I respect their method but it is not mine, especially with noble and cultivated souls like yours. I believe that with such, it is better to point out the evil to them and put the knife in their own hand that they may themselves cut it away.[9]

Jane Chantal testified to this same quality in Francis de Sales' method of dealing with souls: "He was altogether admirable and incomparable in training souls according to their capacity without ever straining them, thus bestowing

[8] H. Burton, *Life of Francis de Sales* (New York: J. P. Kenedy & Sons, 1926) , I, p. 510.
[9] Brémond, *op. cit.*, I, p. 78.

and imprinting on the heart, a certain liberty which set free from all scruple or difficulty." [10]

With this intimate confidence in a God who is "more the Father, less the Lord," the appropriate response is strong, steady, quiet, fervent love; not grim, fearful, tremulous cowering, and Francis' method encourages just such a response. The whole approach stands in striking contrast to Jansenism and to the Pascal of the *Provincial Letters* with his Port Royal thunderbolts that lashed out at "easy virtue," painted the sky livid with God's angry justice, and threatened to strike dead all the sin-sodden generation who did not bow under a stern puritanical code of penitential morals.

A Devotion for All Conditions

Francis de Sales applies this confidence in God and man by freely declaring that the devout life is open and accessible to all types of men and women. "There is no natural temperament so good that it may not be made evil by vicious habits; there is no natural temperament so refractory that it may not, first by the Grace of God and then by industry and diligence be subdued and overcome." [11]

Francis would go further then to insist that God drew those of all temperaments to the life of devotion. He would invite to it, as the great Third Orders had always done, those who now live and who will continue to live and participate in the responsibilities of the active world.

Those who have treated of devotion have almost all had in mind the instruction of persons very much withdrawn from the society of the world or at all events they have taught a kind of devotion which leads to this complete withdrawal. My intention is to instruct those who live in towns, in households, at the

[10] *Ibid.,* II, p. 402.
[11] *Introduction to the Devout Life,* p. 49.

court . . . who very often are not willing even to think of undertaking the devout life while living in the midst of the worldly occupations. . . . It is true that this is not an easy task, and for this reason I should like many to undertake it with more zeal than has been shown up to the present; and therefore wholly weak though I be, I am endeavouring by means of this book to contribute some help to those who, with a generous heart, are willing to undertake this worthy enterprise.[12]

Here is a confidence in the penetrating power of God's love that is prepared to emphasize the accessibility of every pore of the dough of common life to the action of the heavenly yeast and a free assertion of the universal spiritual truth that God is no respecter of favored stations in the sharing of his hidden life.

There is an incident which Tagore mentions in one of his letters to his friend C. F. Andrews in which he describes how in a slum of a great Indian city close to the crying needs of the poor, an intense inward tendering broke through within him, an experience so infinitely precious that he changed all plans and set out for a Himalayan retreat to ponder the experience. As he passed out of the gates of the city, however, the Presence left him and did not return.[13] A wise old Desert Father speaking of the life of devotion once declared, "It is better to have many about thee and to live the solitary life in thy will, than to be alone, and the desire of thy mind be with the crowd."

Francis who knew the *Institutes* of Cassian intimately and in his *Spiritual Conferences* refers more than once to Cassian's own violent outbursts of anger when living in solitude, sums up this encouragement to lay devotion in an opening chapter of the *Introduction*. "It has happened that

[12] *Ibid.*, pp. xxiii–xxiv.
[13] C. F. Andrews, *Letters to a Friend* (London: George Allen & Unwin Ltd., 1928) , pp. 25–26.

many have lost perfection in solitude which notwithstanding is favorable to perfection, and have preserved it amidst a multitude which seems so little favorable to perfection." [14]

"Agility . . . in the Service of God"

What, then, is this devotion which Francis believes men of every temperament and every vocation capable of and which it is the task of the *Introduction* to help to encourage and to nurture? No one has ever expressed more attractively the nature of the devout life than Francis when he says:

Devotion is simply the promptitude, fervour, affection and agility which we have in the service of God. And there is a difference between a good man and a devout man; for he is a good man who keeps the commandments of God, although it be without great promptitude or fervour; but he is devout who not only observes them but does so willingly, promptly and with a good heart.[15]

Only one who is in love, only one who cares, only one who is disrobing himself of self-indulgence can run like that, can serve with that quality of nimbleness. "Ostriches [sinners] never fly; fowls [good persons] fly, but heavily, low down and seldom; but eagles, doves and swallows [devout persons] fly often swiftly and on high." [16] This quality of promptitude and agility he refers to again and again. In the *Conferences* he says, "a loving heart is not content with doing what is ordered, or what seems to be desired, but must do it promptly. It cannot too quickly accomplish what is commanded that it may be free to receive some fresh order." [17] This he opposes to sloth or sadness which is always a return to self-indulgence.

[14] *Introduction*, pp. 9–10.
[15] *Ibid.*, pp. 4–5.
[16] *Ibid.*, p. 4.
[17] *Spiritual Conferences*, p. 188.

Constancy in Devotion

On the other hand, he is equally clear that the truest test of devotion is whether it is still performed with agility when the inward sweetness is withdrawn and when pain and suffering replace them. Using his favorite figure of the bees from which more analogies are drawn in the *Introduction* than from any other source, he says:

For as the bees, when surprised by the wind in the fields lay hold of little stones that they may be able to keep their balance in the air and not be so easily carried away by the storm, so our soul, having resolutely embraced the precious love of God remains constant in the midst of inconstancy and vicissitude of consolations and affections temporal as well as spiritual, exterior as well as interior.[18]

The devotion Francis sets forth is for the long pull of life. It is not based on crisis theology nor is it a crisis devotion. It is one that is possible with God's help to be lived day in and day out until this life is over and then continued with even less resistance forever, for "to serve God is to reign." It is "a constant resolute, prompt, active will to do what is pleasing to God." [19] It is not for the first fortnight after the evangelistic meetings are over or after the reading of the book on man's inward crisis, nor is it limited to the brief duration of the April day of the spirit when we feel "the Presence of pleasure, sweetness, consolation and sensible tenderness of heart which provokes us to tears and sighs, and gives us a certain agreeable and pleasant satisfaction in some spiritual exercises." [20] It is rather perseverance in this devotion through life that matters, the

18 *Introduction*, p. 265.
19 *Ibid.*, p. 266.
20 *Ibid.*, p. 265.

building of the deep habits of obedience into the very pattern of our being, the education of the will.

After telling of how a beloved Desert Father named Jonas who gave himself to a lifetime of matmaking as an act of devotion to God was at last found dead with his legs crossed and his mat stretched above them, Francis adds, "He died doing what he had been doing all his life. It is an act of great humility to go on all our lives doing from obedience one same and mean work, tempted possibly to think we are quite capable of greater things." [21]

Now by focusing on this devotion to God as the goal of the Christian life, Francis has cut through to something universal that transcends all forms of worship, all systems of thought, all problems of religious organization and authority. Not that he regards these as of no importance. That would be far from the truth, for he stood firmly and joyously within the Roman Catholic communion which had an extremely fixed form of worship, theology, and system of ecclesiastical authority. Yet Francis de Sales' point of focus lays on his own church and on every church a goal that is not an exclusive but a common goal, the goal of quickening their members to respond to God's love by a life of devotion. When ecumenical conferences have exhausted their ingenuity in trying vainly to reconcile their diverse forms of worship, their conflicting theologies, and their widely varying types of church authority and polity, there is still a plane on which they might find common ground. It is at that point that the spirit of Francis de Sales might well be invoked to commend to them the fruitful meeting place to be found in the cultivation of this life of devotion: this love of Christ that quickens in us a swift, agile service of God. For whether it is Port Royal or the Order of the Visitation, Methodist or Baptist, Anglican or Quaker, this life of devotion is common coin of the realm.

[21] *Conferences*, p. 167.

Repentance and Devotion

Father Faber after completing a brilliant lecture on the Ignatian method to which he declared that he owed his own salvation, added the words, "but thank God it is not the only way." Certainly that must be said of the Salesian method: it is a good way, but it is not the only way.

What, then, was Francis' way of nurturing one who although living in the world aspired to the *devout* as distinguished from the *good* life? Francis' first counsel was a break with our self-indulgent life and to that end an examination and confession of the life-history of the principal sins committed up to that point. Gentle as Francis' method may be by reputation, its edge is sharp and it cuts deep incisions into life. Sin and indulgent living must go if the devout life is to come.

Stags when they have put on too much flesh, withdraw and retire into their thickets, knowing that their fat is such a burden to them that they are not fit to run, should they chance to be attacked; so also the heart of man burdening itself with the useless, superfluous and dangerous affections cannot run after God readily, freely, and easily which is the true mark of devotion.[22]

This confession of sin and indulgence is to be carried out in the presence of God and if possible of some counselor, with a sharp and bitter revulsion against our sins as cutting us off from God and a commitment to a new way of life. As a means of aid to this uprooting, this driving out of sin and of the affection for sin, Francis proposes a carefully planned cycle of meditations of presumably an hour each for the purpose of loosening, arousing, and preparing the soul for the general confession. By a meditation, Francis

[22] *Introduction*, p. 48.

means the careful guiding of the mind over a set theme, pondering it, weighing it, relating it to your own life and finding its bearing on your future course of life. "Meditation is no other thing than an attentive thought, voluntarily reiterated or entertained in the mind, to excite the will to holy and salutary affections and resolutions." [23]

This process of relating a theme to our own lives in meditation cannot be overemphasized. It is not enough to give a mild *nihil obstat* to truth. If it is to change our lives, if it is to move back into the layer of vital axioms which really determine our choices, it must be a truth *for me*. Therefore in a meditation it is important for the one meditating to ask himself continually what God is trying to say to him through that truth. He must ask, too, what changes that truth will require of his life. We have been so brought up to read and study with a view simply to be familiar with and to be able to remember the content of what we have read, that it is of the sharpest importance that we see that reading and study are not in themselves meditation. Reading may furnish us with material for meditation and study may further clarify this as a preparative for meditating, but meditation itself is a stage beyond understanding what has been presented. Meditation brings us into an encounter, a taking position toward, a coming into personal change by reason of that which we meditate upon. If this is borne in mind the systematic proposals of Francis de Sales which will be generously cited in what follows will have considerably more meaning.

The *Introduction,* then, proposes a series of the loosening, detaching meditations which are to be carried out by taking an hour early in the morning for each and using one a day for ten days. They focus upon both the positive and

[23] *Treatise,* p. 236.

the negative, and the order is most important. For only as they have clearly faced the nature of God and His holy work of creation do they turn to the hindrances to this work by which men have "set at naught their life's design."

These ten subjects for meditation as proposed by Francis give a significant glimpse into his method. Seekers were advised to meditate on creation, on the end for which we are created, of the benefits of God, of sin, of death, of the judgment, of hell, of paradise, of choice of paradise, of the choice the soul makes of the devout life.

These loosening meditations are designed to prepare a person to confess and to do it not by any morbid brooding over past sins but by opening wide the heart as it is confronted by these subjects so that sin may drain out and God's healing forgiveness stream in.

The precise method of making the meditation which Francis recommends is thoroughly Ignatian and seems to have been borrowed straight from the *Spiritual Exercises* in almost every detail. The Ignatian enlistment of the use of the five senses is implied. The holy scene of the Passion is strongly recommended as one in which to place oneself in the frame of as one meditates. To make the meditation on creation or sin or on one's own approaching death at the foot of the cross, beneath the feet of the bleeding crucified one, is to add to its poignancy and add to its compelling us to abandon neutrality and drifting and to take up a position toward that on which we meditate.

Given these purging meditations and a willingness to face and abandon conscious sin as the first step in the cultivation of the life of devotion, Francis declares that "above all I recommend to you *prayer* of the mind and heart" as the living heart of the practice of the devout life. For prayer is in its essence devotion, and without the regular practice of prayer, all devotion will ultimately languish.

Inasmuch as prayer places understanding in the clearness of the divine light, and exposes our will to the warmth of the heavenly love, there is nothing which so purges our understanding of its ignorance and our will of its depraved inclinations. It is the water of benediction, which, when our souls are watered therewith, makes the plants of our good desires revive and flourish, cleanses our souls of imperfections, and quenches the thirst caused by the passion of our hearts.[24]

and without its daily use, Francis might have added, the plant of devotion will slowly shrivel and wither and die.

Over the long range, Francis like all spiritual guides is blunt: No prayer, no devotion. But Francis, being a wise guide knew well enough that the mere recommendation of prayer of the mind and heart is not enough for a beginner. Seeds and a spade and a piece of earth may be enough for a man possessed of a native bent for gardening. But most persons need a gardeners' handbook as well. Therefore he supplies a certain routine of prayer which, practiced day after day, will help to nurture a prayer life that will not become subjective or trivial and be swept away when the first dry times come.

Instruction in Private Prayer

Yet anyone who makes such suggestions is at once open to withering criticism. For he is seeking to train and guide something which at its truest is so infinitely spontaneous, simple and personal as to elude any possible trellis that may have been erected for it. Francis de Sales knows this. He never confuses the trellis with the vine nor his method with real prayer. He knows, however, that some will make this mistake and, viewing the gaunt, empty lattice of the trellis, will repudiate the whole spiritual life as an artificial con-

[24] *Introduction*, p. 53.

struction. It is a risk he is prepared to take, however, knowing the alternative risk of beginners in prayer who are
without counsel.

Now these instructions in prayer which Francis gives
must in the nature of things resemble meditation, for they,
too, are a consciously presented direction to the mind. And
in the *Introduction to the Devout Life* more is said of
meditation than of the deeper ranges of prayer, and often
enough Francis uses the terms "meditation" and "prayer"
almost interchangeably. Yet even in the *Introduction* a
difference in range at least is indicated when Francis says:
"If while saying vocal prayers you feel your heart drawn
and invited to interior or mental prayer, do not resist this
attraction, but allow your mind to go gently in that direction." [25] In the same way, if, as we are not speaking aloud
but are inwardly exhorting ourselves or moving through the
inward Salesian routine of prayer, there should come this
tendering, Francis says: "It may happen that immediately
after the preparation you will find your affection stirred
up towards God: there, Philothea, you must give it the
reins without trying to follow the method which I have given
you." [26] These deepest ranges of prayer which are often
called recollection or contemplation, differ in one sense from
meditation or any routine of prayer by their involuntary
character: they no longer call for effort on our part. Francis
quotes Theresa of Ávila with approval on this point of difference: "He who has written that the prayer of recollection
is made as when a tortoise draws within itself, said well,
saving that these beasts draw themselves in when they please,
whereas recollection is not in our will, but comes to us only
when it pleases God to do us this grace." [27] In addition to

[25] *Ibid.*, p. 55.
[26] *Ibid.*, p. 65.
[27] *Treatise*, p. 351.

this involuntary feature about real contemplation, it also differs from meditation in that there is no longer a focusing on the "piece by piece" details but a sweep into the unity of the whole, and there is the effortless infusion of love which the object seems to bring about.

Francis in his *Treatise on the Love of God* describes with peculiar beauty this deepest state of recollection.

Now this quiet, in which the will works not save only by a simple acquiescence in the divine good pleasure, willing to be in prayer without any other aim than to be in the sight of God according as it shall please Him, is a sovereignly excellent quiet because it has no mixture of self-interest, the faculties of the soul taking no content in it, nor even the will save by its supreme point, in which its contentment is to admit no other contentment but that of being without contentment for the love of the contentment and good pleasure of its God, in which it rests. For, in fine, the height of love's ecstasy is to have will not in its own contentment, but in God's or, not to have contentment in our own will but in God's.[28]

He refers to it again: "He who prays fervently knows not whether he prays or not, for he is not thinking of the prayer which he makes, but of God, to whom he makes it. He that is in the heat of sacred love does not turn his heart back upon himself to see what he is doing, but keeps it set and bent upon God, to whom he applies his love." [29]

But this intimation of the deepest stage of recollection in prayer is beyond the range of experience discussed in the *Introduction,* which Francis regarded as a beginner's handbook. And Francis is most careful to point out that such a level of prayer is never an accomplishment or an earned state but a gift of God which he may bestow on a beginner as well as on a seasoned veteran of prayer or upon neither

[28] *Ibid.,* p. 264.
[29] *Ibid.,* p. 391.

at his good pleasure. The method of prayer, therefore, like the life of devotion, is never regarded as a way of acquiring merit or as a science that must get certain results. It is rather a way of purification in which a man seeks to eliminate some of the blockages of sin and inattention, to hinder the hindrances in order to love God more truly.

We all know the novice's query "How long shall I pray?" and the veteran's answer "long enough to forget time." Francis' directions for a method of prayer for the person living in the world, however, are prefaced by directions to spend an hour in meditation every day, preferably early in the morning, when we are less distracted and more refreshed by sleep. Knowing the distractions of most homes and the danger of disturbance there, he recommends making it in a nearby church if possible "because, moreover, neither father nor mother nor wife nor husband nor anyone can well hinder you from spending an hour in a church." [30] If you should miss this time of prayer, it may be made up by multiplying the swift little cries to God during the day, by reading some book of devotions, together with some penance and a resolve to resume the practice the next day.

Begin by Realizing the Presence of God

It is said that Ignatius of Loyola used to pause outside of a church before entering it and to remember into whose presence he was about to come. Francis incorporates this act of reverence and makes it his first and highly characteristic instruction and help to the novice in prayer: "Begin all your prayers, be they mental or vocal, with the presence of God, and make no exception to this rule, and you will soon perceive how profitable it will be to you." [31] This may be done by arousing yourself to the realization that God is every-

[30] *Introduction*, p. 54.
[31] *Ibid.*, p. 54.

where, and that there is no place in the world where he is not. "When, therefore, you come to prayer, you must say with all your heart, and to your heart, 'O my heart, my heart, God is truly here.' " [32] It may also be effected by reminding yourself that God is not only here but that he is here in a very special manner in your heart and spirit as the heart of your heart. Another way of realizing this presence is to remember that Jesus looks down upon those raised to him in prayer. Picture him and realize the lines of the Song of Songs which declares, "Behold, he standeth behind our wall, looking through the windows, holding the lattices." Francis leans upon Ignatius again for a fourth way and suggests the use of the imagination to represent Jesus in some scene of his sacred humanity and picture yourself there before him. "You will make use, then, of one of these four ways of putting your soul in the presence of God, before prayer; and you must not seek to make use of them all together, but only one at a time, and that briefly and simply." [33]

This instruction has been of enormous help to many a newcomer to mental prayer, who, if he stopped praying aloud, found himself baffled, caught in a swirl of distracting thoughts, and did not know what to do. Francis has also given sufficient variety of suggestions to enable each person to find his most natural form or to allow room for occasional variation.

The invocation is the second step in the instruction. This is simply a prayer which calls upon God for his assistance in the making of the prayer: "Your soul, having realized that she is in the presence of God, prostrates herself with profound reverence, acknowledging her unworthiness . . . asks

[32] *Ibid.*, p. 57.
[33] *Ibid.*, p. 58.

of him the grace to serve him well and to adore him in this meditation." [34]

The third step is again the Ignatian method by which the subject of our meditation is framed or focused through some scene from Christ's life or Passion and through making full use of our five senses and of our imaginative powers in presenting the scene with ourselves placed within it.

For example, if you wish to meditate upon our Saviour on the Cross, you will imagine yourself to be on Mt. Calvary and that you see there all that was done and said on the day of the Passion; or you will imagine the crucifixion as taking place on the very spot where you are. . . . By means of this imaginary scene we confine the spirit within the mystery upon which we intend to meditate, so that it may not range hither and thither, just as we confine a bird within a cage.[35]

The fourth step, he calls the Considerations, the "what in this applies to me" aspects, where not the imagination but the understanding is now brought into play. His instructions are for us to find some consideration that applies to our own life within this scene which we have set for ourselves in this prayer, and to

stay there without passing on to another, acting like the bees, who do not leave the flower so long as they find any honey there to gather. But if you do not find anything to your liking in one of these considerations after having dealt with it and tried it for a little while, pass on to another; but proceed quite gently and simply in the matter, without undue haste.[36]

The fifth step is the application of hatred of our own sin and the outpouring of the love to God and our neighbors

[34] *Ibid.*, p. 59.
[35] *Ibid.*, p. 60.
[36] *Ibid.*, pp. 61-2.

that have arisen within the meditation and then the moving on over into special and particular resolutions for our correction and improvement.

The sixth step as the meditation is brought to a close is the act of thanksgiving to God for the affections and resolutions which he has given us in this meditation.

This is to be followed by an awareness of our being lifted up by God's having reached through to our humanity in his holy sacrificial love in the Incarnation and the offer of our own affections and resolutions to him in this redemptive vessel he has given us.

The prayer is brought to a close by an act of petition to God to bless our affections and resolutions so that we may be faithful to them in practice and to enter into intercessory prayer for our church, our pastors, our friends, our relatives, those who suffer, commending all to the continuous intercession of the saints and closing with the Lord's Prayer, which links us to faithful Christians everywhere.

End with a Spiritual Bouquet

To all of this, Francis de Sales adds his version of the Ignatian colloquy, which he calls by the delightful name of a spiritual nosegay. I climbed an Austrian mountain one morning many years ago and in the grass on the high plateau at its top I gathered a tiny bouquet of the most vividly colored flowers with a rare fragrance. On my table in the pension room in the valley I had only to glance at them to have the beauty of the heights return to me. Francis puts the parable most aptly. "Those who have been walking in a beautiful garden do not leave it willingly without taking away with them four or five flowers, in order to inhale their perfume and carry them about during the day." [37] In like

[37] *Ibid.*, pp. 63–4.

manner Francis counsels that at the conclusion of our prayer, either staying where we are, or walking about for a little while afterward, we select one or two or three points of our meditation that we relish and need for our advancement and select them to come back to again and again during the day to inhale their perfume spiritually. We are then to gather such a spiritual nosegay before leaving the place of prayer and to return to it during the day.

Now these nine steps are very arbitrary, very formal, very laden with architectonic, and each person will find after practice many natural variations of his own. Thanksgiving, awareness of God's work of redemptive love, petition and intercession may quite naturally charge through our considerations and affections and, as mentioned earlier, we may be drawn to affection early in the prayer. Many considerations exclude the possibility of a being placed by the imagination in a sacred setting. This is all very natural, and Francis has only given these arbitrary instructions for beginners. But he does add a wise note when he says, "Until such time as God may raise you higher, I counsel you, Philothea, to remain in the low valley which I have shown you." [38]

Francis is especially persistent in binding the whole prayer to the life of the day. "For example, if I have resolved to win by gentleness the hearts of those who offend me, I will seek that very day an opportunity of meeting them in order to greet them amicably; if I fail to meet them, I will at least try to speak well of them and pray to God on their behalf." [39] Francis cautions Philothea against lurching from such a time of prayer into the "rush and run" school of life, yet he warns her that unless the fifth point of the meditation, that covers specific resolutions such as those

[38] *Ibid.*, p. 61.
[39] *Ibid.*, p. 65.

examples just mentioned, is then carried out into life it will poison future prayer.

On Moving from Prayer to Life

His words on this transition from prayer to life are apt:

You must even accustom yourself to know how to pass from prayer to all sorts of actions which your vocation and profession justly and lawfully requires of you, though they seem very far removed from the affections which you have received in prayer. I mean that the advocate must learn to pass from prayer to pleading, the merchant to business; the married woman to the duties of her state and to the cares of the household, with so much gentleness and tranquillity that the spirit be not disturbed thereby; for, since both are according to the will of God, we must make the passage from the one to the other in a spirit of humility and devotion.[40]

His shrewd observations as to the effect upon others of this devotional life when applied to our common life are worthy of noting. Few passages are more characteristic of Salesian piety than where he observes:

Sick people will love your devotion if they are comforted in a charitable manner; your family if it recognizes that you are more careful of its concerns, gentler in the emergencies of everyday life, more sympathetic in your method of correcting, and so on; your husband if he sees that with the growth of your piety you are more affectionate towards him and sweeter in the love you show him; your relations and friends if they see in you more sincerity, more agreement with such of their wishes as are not contrary to those of God. Briefly, we should as far as possible make our piety attractive.[41]

In addition to this daily period of meditation, Francis counsels a prayer upon awakening in which God is thanked

[40] *Ibid.*, p. 65.
[41] Burton, *op. cit.*, I, p. 416.

for preservation through the night, the approaching day is thought of and received as a gift and resolutions made for its good use, the affairs in prospect for the day are quickly scanned in God's presence, and God's help asked for strength to meet them. In like fashion he suggests that before we go to bed at night there should be an examination of conscience thanking God for any good we have done and asking his forgiveness for our evil, commending those we love to his care and committing ourselves to his care for the night. "This exercise," writes Francis, "like that of the morning, must never be forgotten; for by the morning exercises you open the windows of your soul to the Sun of Justice, and by that of the evening you close them again against the powers of darkness." [42]

But this is not all, for Francis would have the devout soul withdraw inwardly and recall its spirit to the presence of God again and again through the day by inward cries of, "Why dost Thou think of me so often, my Lord, and why do I think so seldom of Thee?" or "Where are we, oh my soul?" He counsels the making of "many withdrawals into the solitude of your heart, whilst you are outwardly in the midst of intercourse or business." Beyond this frequent inward retirement he suggests the use of ejaculatory prayers, those short, ardent prayers for help, or thankfulness, or of abandonment. "Plant them in your soul as a standard and make a thousand different movements of your heart to give yourself the love of God." [43] Just as men who are in love turn their thoughts often to their loved one in the midst of other occupations, "so those who love God cannot cease to think of him, long for him, aspire to him, and speak of him."

[42] *Introduction*, p. 71.
[43] *Ibid.*, p. 74.

. . . Now in this exercise of spiritual retirement and ejaculatory prayers lies the great work of devotion: it can supply the
lack of all other prayers, but the failure of this can scarcely
be made good by any other means. Without it the contemplative
life cannot be properly followed, nor the active life lived otherwise than ill; without it repose is but idleness, and work but
embarrassment; and therefore, I beseech you, embrace it with
your whole heart and never abandon it.[44]

Inward Drought and Prayer

Francis is careful to warn Philothea of the dry times that
will come in prayer, those periods when all prayer is un-
real, when we find ourself in the valley of dry bones, when
our whole religious venture may seem to be a childish
illusion undertaken in one of our moments of sentimental
weakness. The usual beginner stops praying at such a time
and says in explanation that he no longer feels in the mood
to pray. For one in this condition Francis proposes a mild
shock treatment to stir up the person's religious life if that
should be all that is needed, and advises, as does Augustine
Baker, a turning from mental to vocal prayers to God in
order to arouse the soul. At other times he counsels the
reading of a devotional book with close attention or the use
of some posture of devotion like prostrating yourself on the
ground or embracing a cross. Yet, often enough, these
artificial stimuli have no effect whatever, and then Francis
counsels steady continuance in exercises of devotion, suggesting that these exercises are of even more value then than
at any other time, for they reveal to God and ourselves
that our devotion is no fair-weather affair during the time
our heart is full of tender consolations, but that in all sea-
sons we are at God's disposal.

"Nothing is so useful, nothing so profitable in such dry-

44 *Ibid.*, pp. 77-9.

ness and barrenness as to have no attachment to the desire of being delivered from it." [45] "Work on faithfully," he writes to Madame de la Flechere, "with the farthest point of your will, amidst this darkness and dryness: one ounce of work done in this way is worth more than a hundred of that which is done amidst consolations and feelings, and although that state is sweeter, nevertheless this is better." [46] Again he notes:

It is no great thing to serve a prince in the quietness of a time of peace, and amidst the pleasures of court, but to serve him in the hardships of war, amidst troubles and persecutions, is a true mark of constancy and fidelity. . . . Finally, Philothea, in the midst of all our dryness and barrenness, let us not lose courage, but whilst patiently awaiting the return of consolations, let us always pursue the even tenor of our way; let us not omit any of our exercises of devotion, but rather, if it be possible, let us multiply our good works and, since we cannot present succulent comfits to our dear spouse, let us give him dried ones, for it is all one to him, provided the heart that offers them to him is perfectly steadfast in its will to love him.[47]

Francis of course presupposes the regular practice of corporate worship and the sacramental life and adds a suggestion that Philothea "have always at hand some good book of devotion . . . and read a little of it every day with great devotion, as though you were reading missives sent to you by the Saints from Heaven to show you the way there and to give you the courage to take it." [48] He also commends those who make retreats of some days, that "they may stir up their souls by divers spiritual exercises to the entire reformation of their life." [49] When he became a

[45] *Ibid.*, p. 274.
[46] Scott, *op. cit.*, p. 266.
[47] *Introduction*, pp. 275–6.
[48] *Ibid.*, p. 85.
[49] *Treatise*, p. 544.

bishop, he resolved to make an annual retreat of eight days and faithfully carried out this intention.

By far the greater bulk of the *Introduction* is given over to moral counsel. On this account one critic has accused Francis of being little more than a French Epictetus. But one who would see in this moral counsel only a detached system of French stoicism, has regarded it in a most superficial way. For, from the advice about attendance at balls, card playing and flirtation to the treatment of detraction, of patience with ourselves and of the bearing of affliction, each counsel is directed with a view of how the practice discussed will affect the devout one's swift and loving obedience to God. And the utter lack of a grim, puritanical attitude, together with a desire for a joyous life in which all the faculties were refreshed and supple in the service of God is intimately related to the deep Christian faith in a God of love in whose service is perfect freedom.

I do not believe this glimpse of the *Introduction* could be better brought to a close than by a reference again to the humility of one engaged on the course of this swift obedience to God. I know of nowhere that Salesian humility is better stated than in the closing chapter of the *Introduction to the Devout Life,* when Francis counsels Philothea to nail her colors to the mast and openly to admit that she is trying to live the devout life. "And if anyone should say to you that one can live devoutly without the practice of these counsels and exercises, do not deny it; but reply graciously that your weakness is so great that you have need of more assistance than others."

3

The *Journal* of John Woolman

CHAPTER 3

The *Journal* of John Woolman

JOHN WOOLMAN'S *Journal* is an eighteenth-century autobiography of singular power. In all its homespun modesty, it reveals the heroic example of a spiritually guided and centered life that was poured out in self-spending service to a dispossessed group, the Negroes, whose condition of slavery mocked the Christian profession of the time. I would not hesitate to call the moving life which this unusual diary records, the life of an American saint.

I still persist in using that term "American saint" although I well remember the rebuke it once brought from a devout Continental woman when I asked her some fifteen years ago if America might not be led to a deeper religious life by the appearance of a saint. She smiled tolerantly and shook her head as she explained to me that it took centuries of deep religious tradition to produce that confidence and sureness of stroke that marked a saint and that in the shallow religious life of turbulent and explosive, adolescent America we could not expect any such figure to appear. A few centuries hence, perhaps, but until now, or in the years just ahead— *ausgeschlossen*.

Her remark had the chastening flavor of a story the English enjoy telling of a wealthy American who appeared at St. John's College in Oxford and who, being fascinated by the wonderful turf of the St. John's College garden, slipped a five-pound note into the head gardener's hand and asked him to tell him how he could grow such grass as that on his place in America. The gardener pocketed the note and told him that it was really quite simple, that all you had to do was to seed and water and roll it faithfully for four hundred years.

Yet in spite of all theories, and in spite of our slender stock of tradition as the Old World calculates it, an authentic saint named John Woolman did appear in America at the beginning of the second century of its settlement. He was born in 1720 and became a part of a third-generation Quaker community near Burlington, New Jersey. The founder of the Quakers, George Fox, had only begun his preaching in England seventy years before, and William Penn, the Quaker statesman, had died in 1718 only two years before this date. Benjamin Franklin was fourteen years old at the time of Woolman's birth, and George Washington was born twelve years after Woolman.

Coming at such a period and in such a setting Woolman was, therefore, the inheritor of a new democratic tradition that had been beaten out on the anvil of Cromwellian England. This tradition was rooted in religion. The sacredness of the individual which it proclaimed did not originally spring from a political rationalization but rather from a sense of his divine worth. The Clarke papers in describing how the humblest private in the Commonwealth army always had access to Cromwell himself, go on to point out that Cromwell had a terrible fear that God might wish to speak to him through some man, and since he did not know who this divine messenger would be, he was bound to treat each man with equal regard. This sense of the com-

mon man as a potential trumpet of God, a potential candle-
stick of the Lord, of man as infinitely precious to God, was
to write itself in rationalized form into the famous Tolera-
tion Acts in 1689. But in the years that immediately preceded 1689, the persecutions under the Restoration drove
many thousands to New Jersey, and after 1682 to Pennsylvania, in order to set up in these two states under Quaker
auspices a civil community governed by laws that were
molded to respect the divine dignity and liberty of the individual person.

It is an interesting fact, as Janet Whitney has pointed
out, that Woolman was born into a community of men and
women who were used to work. The New Jersey and Pennsylvania colonists were different from the Virginia aristo-
crats or the Hudson River traders in that they included a
very large number of skilled farmers and master craftsmen.
Woolman's grandfather had been such a colonist. Woolman's father was an excellent farmer and weaver who was
blessed with a large family. Three of the six girls, Elizabeth, Sarah, and Patience, had preceded John Woolman's
birth, and he was the first of seven sons. The family all
worked and John knew throughout his boyhood what hard
farm labor meant, and as a tailor and an orchard keeper his
whole life is stamped in the mold of one who worked.

He had a good schooling and had ample access to books
both in his own home and in the well-stocked, if somewhat
carefully chosen, libraries of the Quaker families in his
neighborhood, so that there is no evidence to support the
view of Woolman as a poor ignorant boy who received his
culture wholly from within. Amelia Mott Gummere in her
important edition of Woolman's *Journal and Essays* says:

Woolman was a hard reader all his life and when one reflects
upon the intimate friends who loved and admired him, among

whom were the distinguished brothers Pemberton, and the Frenchman Anthony Benezet, only second to John Woolman in the importance of his antislavery work, one becomes somewhat impatient at encountering in every writer on Woolman, the persistent tradition of his illiteracy, linked usually with poverty. That he was neither unlearned nor poor there is abundant evidence. Both impressions have doubtless come from the utter simplicity of the man's life and thought. He speaks of his family as "we who are of a middle station between poverty and riches." [1]

Woolman records: "Read in the evening in Don Quixote . . . in Chambers Dictionary . . . in Desideratus . . . in Sir Thomas More's Utopia . . . in Paradise Lost." [2] This is no log-cabin diet of the Bible and Shakespeare! And in his maturity, as a ledger which was found twenty years ago points out, Woolman possessed such books as the writings of Eusebius, John Everard, Erasmus, and Boehme.

It is, however, proper to note that he seems to have had no higher formal education than the local school afforded and that the rest of his reading was that of an eager mind following its own inner interests and needs. His skill as a drawer of legal documents was in demand from very early manhood on, and in later life he served different periods as a schoolmaster and prepared a grammar that was regarded as very acceptable for school use. There is here a reflection of the healthy respect for the mind and its place in the practical concerns of life that marked an able rural Quaker colonial citizen of this period.

The Religious Background

His parents were practicing Quakers and he notes that "their stability and firmness through a divine blessing is at

[1] Amelia Mott Gunmere, *The Journal and Essays of John Woolman* (New York: The Macmillan Company, 1922), p. 15.

[2] Janet Payne Whitney, *John Woolman* (Boston: Little, Brown & Company, 1942), p. 41.

times like a dew on the tender plants around about them and the weightiness of their spirits secretly left marks on the minds of others." This Quaker family was regular in its attendance at the little Quaker meetinghouse on both Sundays and Thursdays, and John Woolman, like the other children, was taken to meeting and learned there to sit quietly in the midst of the silent prayerful waiting upon the Lord which characterizes the Quaker form of worship.

In the intense stillness of a gathered meeting a child may pursue his own thoughts or count the windowpanes or study flies upon the wall or gaze at some serene face among the ministers and elders who are seated on the slightly elevated facing benches, or eye some other child engaged in the same pastime. But he cannot escape at moments being inwardly sensitized and touched in terms of his own dim formulations of what God is and what his life should be. And this learning to pause, learning to sit quietly and catching the sense of expectancy in those about him, while it may provoke horror in the dynamic religious educators of our day, did produce in a boy like John Woolman a tenderness and a sensitiveness to inward need and to the scruples of conscience and to the direct way to open the life to the inward teacher.

We have only twelve pages in his *Journal* that are devoted to the first thirty-six years in his life before he actually began keeping the *Journal*, but they are full of marks of this growing sensitiveness and of the power of this silence to convict him of his own need. His account of the sharpness of his remorse which followed the time when he killed a mother robin with a stone and then had to go on and kill each of the babes in the nest as he realized that they would starve to death now that he had robbed them of their provider is not, to be sure, as drawn out as the long homily on sin and remorse that accompanies Augustine's account of his own youthful theft of the pears in the *Confessions*.

But the fact that Woolman remembered this incident so clearly at the age of thirty-six is some indication of the tenderness which was begotten in him by this frequent early exposure to the inward instruction which comes in the silence.

There is no possible way of understanding the life of Woolman without a sympathetic grasp of the central place in his life which this openness to God in the silence of the corporate meeting for worship played. Yet this inward sensitiveness in him as a boy was matched with a keen, vigorous, socially attractive nature that was much beloved by his fellows. He described himself in this period: "To exceed in the art of foolish jesting and to promote mirth were my chiefest study," and to one who was as likable and who liked to be liked as much as Woolman in his human way always did, some of the conduct which in his adult life he felt constrained to follow meant no small going against natural inclination, as he so touchingly confesses in the *Journal*.

This early religious nurture in the silent meeting was accompanied by a series of youthful surges toward the religious life which were each followed by a period of backsliding. Yet he persisted and "kept steadily to meetings," and when he was nineteen this inward quickening after so many failures began to guide his life. He wrote of this period: "my heart was tender and often contrite, and universal love to my fellow creatures increased in me." He did not trumpet these things, keeping them sealed up within his own breast, but he forsook his old companions and after much prayer and inward struggle during the next two years, he found his life being shaped more and more from this inward root.

This love for his fellow creatures, Woolman always interpreted to include the animal kingdom. Eastern religious life, especially in Buddhism and Hinduism, has felt this responsibility of men for the pain and suffering which they bring to animals much more keenly than has the Christian religion. In recent years, however, Albert Schweitzer, whose feeling of *reverence for life* is so deep that he will not carelessly snip the head off a daisy with his cane as he walks through a field, has argued the case at great length in his ethical writings. John Woolman states it all in a long sentence:

As the mind was moved by an inward principle to love God as an invisible comprehensible being, so by the same principle it was moved to love Him in all his manifestations in the visible world; that as by His breath the flame of life was kindled in all animal sensible creatures, to say we love God as unseen and at the same time to practice cruelty toward the least creature moving by His life, or by life derived from Him was a contradiction in His life.[3]

This is the argument. But the reality for him as for Francis of Assisi and for Schweitzer was an inward one. His heart had been inwardly enlarged by God toward all creatures, and toward the close of his life he wrote in this vein: "I believe where the love of God is verily perfected, and the true spirit of government watchfully attended to, a tenderness towards all creatures made subject to us will be experienced, and a care felt in us that we do not lessen the sweetness of life in the animal creation which the great Creator intends for them under our government." [4] This tenderness in Woolman toward his fellow creatures everywhere was to set for him his life task as the advocate of men's responsibility before God for this same sweetness of life for their fellow Negroes and fellow Indians as they desired for themselves.

[3] *Journal* (Whittier ed.), p. 58.
[4] *Ibid.*, p. 255.

The *Journal* gives us a good insight into the growth of what Quakers call a "concern" and from Woolman's experience we can learn more about how an inward vocation develops and matures than from any book on psychological counseling that I know. In the first place there is always in the background this sense of his life being at the disposal of God. The regular Quaker practice of corporate worship and of private prayer furnished a means of bringing him "close to the root," as he expressed it. But more important still was this constant attempt on his part to live close to the root, close to the inward teacher, close to the tendering presence that he had known and felt. He tried to let his words, his choice of bread-work, his choice of life partner, his choice of the standard of elegance he was to indulge himself in, his choice of the missions he was to undertake, be open to be decided by the light that came from within.

It is necessary only to realize how important this malleable openness to inward direction was in Woolman's life to begin to have a better insight into the Continental woman's insistence that a saint can only come from an established religious community. For only where there are others who have lived or are living such a life of abandon, is there the encouragement, the expectation, the nurture that prunes away individualistic excess and yet helps give the setting for continual renewal. A man or woman must have this if at one and the same time they are to go beyond the customary compromises and mediocrity of the ordinary life and yet to retain such touch with the heart of the common life as to reveal it to itself for what it might become and to appeal to this common life as a saint has the power of doing. Without such a community or tradition the one who feels called to this deeper devotion may hesitate, falter, or stop short, or he may develop willful eccentricities or grievances which may end by making him only a queer enemy of the people and cut him off from the true life of full devotion.

In spite of the fact that it was scarcely three generations old, the closely knit Quaker community and traditions into which Woolman entered had numbered among it many who had experienced the inner fervor of the divine presence, who had put their lives at the disposal of God, who had traveled to many parts of the world under a sense of concern, who had altered certain areas of social practice in order to bring them more closely into line with the dignity of man as a chosen vehicle of God, and who above all expected that God was continuing to reveal himself to those who waited faithfully upon him and that he would open the way for those who stayed close to the source of this revelation. John Woolman lived in this Quaker community. He was encouraged, sensitized, and shaped by it, and carried out his life mission within its framework. And in turn he quickened and lifted it and helped it to rid itself of certain inner contradictions that marred its witness.

In the second place, all of Woolman's concerns were carried out by one who continued to live in the world, who married and had children, who worked with his hands and who continued throughout to earn his own and his family's living. This, too, was in keeping with the Quaker lay tradition, although the Society was always prepared, if necessary, to assist the family and defray the travel of a person who was released to follow a personal concern. As Janet Whitney has put it: "It would be unreasonable to suppose that the compelling work of God could come only to the well-to-do." For Woolman, however, such help was never necessary. This close linkage to the common life of all men has made Woolman's achievement even more impressive and compelling to our time.

In the third place, the specific social reforms which

Woolman advocated and the methods by which he advanced them never exhausted, and were always secondary, to his witness for the availability of the divine presence and power here and now in this life, and to the connection of that presence with specific practice in this world. Woolman's reforms were only applications of this deeper power and they drew their strength and validity exclusively from it. This prevented him from ever falling the victim of any narrow doctrinaire reformer mentality with two or three *idées fixes* and kept his means of advancing these concerns continually purified. It also gave a deeper rootage and a unity and coherence to all his thinking on social themes.

The Growth of a "Concern"

Against this background, the *Journal* tells the story of the young Woolman coming in from the farm and entering a shop in Mt. Holly, New Jersey, when he was twenty-one. His reliability was such that he was soon running the shop completely during the long absences of his employer. In addition to tending shop he kept the accounts, made out legal conveyances for the convenience of the customers, and several years later began learning the trade of tailoring. By the end of seven years he bought out his employer and had the expanding business to himself.

The owning of Negro slaves in New Jersey at this period was common and little more was thought of it than would be thought of owning and deriving dividends from shares of stock in a business corporation today. Not only were the plantation owners of the South living off the labor of slaves, but many early New England and English fortunes were made out of the handsome profits that were gotten out of shipping through the three-cornered traffic of textiles from England to Africa—slaves from Africa to Virginia—and tobacco from Virginia to England.

There had been scruples in the minds of early Quakers on the matter of slaveholding. Fox had counseled improved treatment of slaves, religious instruction, and the possible freeing of them after a term of service. The early German settlers of Philadelphia had passed resolutions against the holding practice before the seventeenth century was out. But the practice of holding slaves had not been seriously affected by these measures.

John Woolman's uneasiness and concern against slaveholding developed slowly out of the root of this inward love for his fellow creatures. The steps are most instructive to follow. His employer owned a woman slave and one day told him to prepare a bill of sale for a customer who had bought the slave. Woolman's concern was not yet fully clear. He was an employee and his master had ordered it done, and the customer was an elderly member of the Society of Friends. He made out the bill "so through weakness I gave way and wrote it," but he told his employer and the buyer of the slave that he believed that slave-keeping was a practice inconsistent with the Christian religion. On the second occasion, Woolman was better prepared and when asked by a customer to draw up papers for the transfer of a slave, Woolman declined, admitting that many Quakers kept slaves but that he felt the practice to be wrong. The *Journal* records: "I spoke to him in good will and he told me that keeping slaves was not altogether agreeable to his mind; but that the slave being a gift made to his wife he had accepted her." When the occasion arose again, John Woolman with much inward trembling confessed his scruples and refused the request of an elderly Friend. Woolman reports in his *Journal*, however, that "a few days after he came again and directed their freedom, and I then wrote his will."

He was called on to prepare a will for a man suffering

from a bad injury who named the child to whom he wished
to give his young Negro. Woolman writes:

I considered the pain and distress he was in, and knew not
how it would end, so I wrote his will, save only the part concerning his slave, and carrying it to his bedside read it to him.
I then told him in a friendly way that I could not write any instruments by which my fellow-creatures were made slaves, without bringing trouble on my own mind. I let him know that I
charged nothing for what I had done, and desired to be excused
from doing the other part in the way he proposed. We then had
a serious conference on the subject; at length he agreeing to set
her free, I finished his will.[5]

Lest anyone think that this concern, once accepted, was
followed out with ease, Woolman's own words are important
to observe, "As writing is a profitable employ, and as offend-
ing people was disagreeable to my inclination I was strait-
ened in my mind; but as I looked to the Lord, He inclined
my heart to His testimony." [6] Or again: "Tradesmen and re-
tailers of goods who depend upon their business for a living
are naturally inclined to keep the goodwill of their customers; nor is it pleasant for young men to be under any
necessity to question the judgment or honesty of elderly
men, and more especially of such as have a fair reputation." [7]
To this deeply honest confession of the inward resistance
to be overcome, he gives the conclusion of a disregarding
of these factors of self-interest: "I had fresh confirmation
that acting contrary to present outward interest from a
motive of Divine love and in regard to truth and righteous-
ness and thereby incurring the resentments of people, opens
the way to a treasure better than silver, and to a friendship
exceeding the friendship of men." [8]

[5] *Journal*, p. 88.
[6] *Ibid.*, p. 81.
[7] *Ibid.*, p. 86.
[8] *Ibid.*, p. 81.

Personal Exposure Broadens the Concern

But until now Woolman's concern against slaveholding was local in its setting. In his later writings he is a strong advocate of personal exposure as a means of shaking us out of our lethargy and our acquiescence in wrongs which others suffer either at our hands or because we do not help protest them. The Hindu tribe living on the border of Afghanistan which is reported to have a religious scruple against any one of their number taking the life of an animal, but who have arranged to buy meat to eat that has been killed by Mohammedan butchers, would in Woolman's eye be no more in need of introduction to itself than the benevolent Christian Virginian slaveholder who would not himself dream of performing the unbelievable cruelties and bloodshed involved in the slave procurement in Africa and their transport to America, but who would buy them with a clear conscience when they appear in Norfolk.

"Whatever nicety of distinction there may be betwixt going in person on expeditions to catch slaves, and buying those with a view of self-interest which others have taken," wrote Woolman, "it is clear that such a distinction is in words not in substance . . . for were there none to purchase slaves, they who live by stealing and selling them would of consequence do less of it." [9] He also counsels that, "it is good for all those who live in fullness to improve every opportunity of being acquainted with the hardships and fatigues of those who labor for their living, and think seriously with themselves, am I influenced with true charity in fixing my demands.[10]

Woolman owed to this very exposure the deepening and

[9] Gunmere, *op. cit.,* p. 377.
[10] *Ibid.,* p. 406.

broadening of his own concern. In 1746 he secured his meeting's permission, which was given in the form of a written minute commending him to Friends' meetings he would visit and minister to spiritually on his travels, and together with a companion, he traveled down through Virginia and into North Carolina, and in the course of holding religious meetings among the Quakers on his journey he saw with his own eyes the full-blown system of slavery. When Woolman was born there was only one Negro to ten white men in Virginia. Twenty-six years later when Woolman visited Virginia there was one white to one Negro, and in South Carolina one white to fifteen Negroes. Woolman saw these Negro slaves come in from a long, hard day's work in the tobacco fields, receive their small daily issue of corn, go home and grind it and only then be able to prepare their meal to refresh themselves. He knew how tired he was at the end of a day of riding and he contrasted the comfort of the wealthy Quaker planter's house where he received every comfort, to the lot of those who supported the planter by their labor, and reports that he and his companion "were in some degree baptized into a feeling sense of the condition of the people." [11]

When I ate, drank, and lodged free cost with people who lived in ease on the hard labor of their slaves, I felt uneasy . . . and I frequently had conversations with them in private about it. . . . This trade of importing slaves from their native country being much encouraged amongst them and the white people and their children living without much labor was frequently the subject of my serious thoughts. I saw in these southern provinces so many vices and corruptions increased by this trade and this way of life that it appeared to me as a dark gloominess hanging over the land.[12]

[11] *Journal,* p. 70.
[12] *Ibid.,* p. 72.

He returned to Mt. Holly after this three months, strongly moved by this direct exposure and with his concern deepened and broadened. He made a further journey in New Jersey and the following year he was released again by his meeting to travel in the spiritual ministry among Quakers in New England. Here, in the course of his journey he saw the grip of the profitable slave trade upon New England. In the course of making these religious journeys, he had traveled in a single year some two thousand miles. In the years that followed, he continued these visitations now for a month, another time for two, and covered Pennsylvania, New Jersey, and Maryland with some thoroughness.

His testimony on slavery had become articulate now and he was prepared to make family visits to Quakers where the question of their continued ownership of slaves was involved. He visited New England again and became intimate with the Governor's son, Thomas Hazard, who shared his concern over the holding of slaves. He was present at Newport Meeting when a slave ship belonging to one of the Quaker members arrived while Yearly Meeting was in session, and he presented a memorandum on the subject to the Rhode Island state legislature.

In 1757 he made his second journey through the South using a horse and covering some eleven hundred miles in a two months' visitation. Now he knew his mission and, hard as the labor was, he endeavored with God's help to discharge his responsibility in calling the wrongness of keeping slaves to the attention of those he visited.

Means and End

His method was one that was always deeply respectful of those he visited. It presupposed a divine center in them that was open to approach. His task was to answer to that of

God in them. Each visit was personal and was carried on in love, but it went to the point. He declares, "It was my concern from day to day to say neither more nor less than what the spirit of truth opened in me, being jealous over myself lest I should say anything to make my testimony look agreeable to that mind in people which is not in pure obedience to the cross of Christ." [13]

From his important published paper, "Considerations on Keeping Negroes," we can presume that he showed to his hosts and to those who attended the meetings which he appointed, the incongruity of slaveholding and obedience to the cross of Christ. He showed them how it wronged and degraded their brother the Negro. He pointed out the way it undermined their political principles of justice, how painfully it affected their own children to live in ease off the results of others' labor, and how contrary to the design of the Creator it was for themselves to live without labor.

The hospitality of Quakers to their traveling ministers was nowhere more bounteous and warm than in the South and Woolman found it no small task after his hosts had given so generously to him to fulfil his mission that touched so directly upon their whole source of support and style of life.

The *Journal* tells in a restrained way something of the cost of these exercises.

It is good for thee to dwell deep that thou mayest feel and understand the spirits of people. If we believe truth points towards a conference on some subjects in a private way, it is needful for us to take heed that their kindness, their freedom and affability do not hinder us from the Lord's work. I have experienced that in the midst of kindness and smooth conduct, to speak close and home to them who entertain us, on points that relate to outward interest is hard labor. [14]

13 *Journal,* p. 158.
14 *Ibid.,* pp. 168-9.

His conscience was not easy about accepting such hospitality "from what appeared to me to be the gain of oppression," and as he believed "conduct more convincing than language," he labored in inward prayer before this second southern journey and was brought after much struggle to trust that

by his strength I should be enabled even to leave money with the members of society where I had entertainment, when I found that omitting it would obstruct the work I believed had called me. . . . The way in which I did it was thus: When I expected soon to leave a Friend's house where I had entertainment, if I believed that I should not keep clear from gain of oppression without leaving money, I spoke to one of the heads of the family privately and desired them to accept of those pieces of silver, and give them to such of their Negroes as they believed would make best use of them; and at other times I gave them to the Negroes myself, as the way looked clearest to me. Before I came out I provided a large number of small pieces for this purpose and thus offering them to some who appeared to be wealthy people was a trial both to me and to them. But the fear of the Lord so covered me at times that my way was made easier than I expected; and few, if any, manifested any resentment at the offer, and most of them after some conversation accepted of them.[15]

In the next decade, in addition to journeys in Pennsylvania, New Jersey, and New England, he made three journeys southward and made them on foot in order that he might be more completely exposed to the condition of those whose plight affected him so deeply and perhaps share in a small way in their suffering and witness to their masters by his action as well as his words. "To proceed without a horse seemed clearest to me. Though travel on foot was wearisome to my body, yet it was agreeable to the state of mind." Again he is drawn "to travel on foot among

[15] *Ibid.*, pp. 101–2.

them that by so traveling I might have a more lively feeling of the condition of the oppressed slaves," and he reports both the bodily weakness and discouragement that overtook him on the hot, dry journey and the wave of thankfulness to the gracious Father as he was inwardly renewed. "My heart was often tendered under the divine influence and enlarged in love towards the people among whom we travelled." [16]

Voluntary Simplicity

Throughout this unfolding of a concern that grew on and on in Woolman until it took him to his death, he lived his normal round of life in business and farming. After setting up for himself in 1747, he found his tailoring and dry goods establishment rapidly expanding as Mt. Holly grew and prospered. He had learned the tailoring trade and chosen this type of establishment as a trade that would enable him "so to pass my time that nothing would hinder me from the most steady attention to the voice of the true shepherd." He had had several offers of business that looked profitable, "but there appeared too great a share of cumber to attend to it," and he had rejected them in order to get a life "pretty free from much cumber," even though the income was small. Woolman steadily advised poor customers to take less expensive goods that would be more useful to them, and his whole attitude toward his business was in sharp contrast to the merchant mentality of his day.

Woolman wanted freedom to follow the inward guide and saw wealth as a great distraction of mind. As his little business expanded "the way to large business appeared open," but Woolman at that point began cutting it down by stocking fewer and fewer articles until little remained except his tailoring and his small eleven-acre orchard and

[16] *Ibid.*, p. 215.

garden and house which he had purchased. His goal was complete self-support but "a life so plain that a little suffices," and it was on this base that he lived the rest of his life.

In 1749 he married Sarah Ellis and the *Journal* is painfully brief on the circumstances. It records only: "The Lord was pleased to give me a well-inclined damsel, Sarah Ellis, to whom I was married the 18th day of 8th. month, 1749." Janet Whitney proves that even this brief entry is an insertion in the Swarthmore manuscript to meet the criticisms of friends who noted the omission. Yet there is every evidence that this omission was dictated from modesty about the affairs of his private life, for there are ample signs throughout Woolman's letters that their family life was especially happy and tender. Although his wife was frail, a daughter, Mary, was born a year and a half after the marriage. She was a great joy to her father and became the wife of John Comfort and the mother of ten children, seven of whom were sons. A little son was born to Sarah Woolman in 1753, but he lived only a few months.

The Quaker family tradition that acknowledges the love of a man and woman as ever obedient to the divine command and leaves each member free to follow the calls of the inward guide, was clearly in evidence in Sarah's patient willingness for John Woolman to make the journeys he felt inwardly called upon to undertake. William Penn's testimony to his wife Guilielma's readiness, in spite of her frail health, for him to cross the ocean alone when it seemed right for him to go, could well have been said of Sarah Woolman. Penn declared, "She would not suffer me to neglect any public meeting after I got my liberty upon her account, saying often, 'O my dearest! Don't hinder any Good for me. I desire thee go: I have cast my care upon the Lord: I shall see thee again!' " It was in this tradition of

Quaker marriage that Sarah Woolman stood, and without it John Woolman's way would not have been open to him.

"Following the Leadings of Truth"

With the frontiers dotted with incidents of fighting between Indians and whites, Woolman in 1762 felt a drawing to witness to a loving concern for the Indians whom he felt were being so badly mistreated, by making a visit to a group of them, some of whom he had personally met in Philadelphia, but who lived in a village on the upper Susquehanna. His statement of his concern to visit them is classic, and might well become the motto of the Christian missionary motivation of the future. "Love was the first motion, and thence a concern arose to spend some time with the Indians, that I might feel and understand their life and the spirit they live in, if happily I might receive some instruction from them, or they might be in any degree helped forward by my following the leadings of truth among them." [17]

Travel was difficult at that season and with the troubles of war increasing it was a dangerous undertaking. On the very night of his departure, word came through of the capture of a fort west of Pittsburgh and of the scalping of a number of the English. Woolman pondered the matter: "My heart was turned to the Lord that no motion might in the least degree be attended to but that of the pure spirit of truth." [18] But he decided to set out.

In the course of the journey in company with his companion, Benjamin Parvin, for the Quakers nearly always traveled in pairs, he saw much evidence of the chicanery and the shrewd use of liquor by which the whites often took from the Indians "their skins and furs gotten through

[17] *Journal,* p. 192.
[18] *Ibid.,* p. 187.

much fatigue and hard travels in hunting . . . and afterward when they suffer for want of the necessaries of life [the Indians] are angry with those who for the sake of gain, took advantage of their weakness." [19]

He tells in such human fashion in the *Journal* of a night he spent in great agony of mind as to whether he was continuing on this dangerous journey really at the guidance of the inward teacher or simply for fear of the ridicule he might receive for his cowardice if he turned back. To less sensitive souls who suffer inward questionings long after they believe they have followed the way they were inwardly directed, it is a great consolation to know that late in his life so devoted a servant of God as Woolman was not immune to such a reopening of his original decision. He wrote of its outcome: "Full of these thoughts, I lay the greater part of the night while my beloved companion slept by me till the Lord, my gracious Father, Who saw the conflicts of my soul was pleased to give quietness. Then I was again strengthened to commit my life, and all things relating thereto, into His heavenly hands, and got a little sleep towards day." [20]

Woolman's visit at the Indian village of Wehaloosing culminated in a final silent meeting for worship with the Indians. Toward the end of it Woolman rose to pray, and an interpreter stood up beside him to translate his words into the Indian tongue. Woolman begged him to sit down and prayed a moving prayer in English. After the meeting the Indian chief Papunehang, being much tendered by the meeting, told Woolman through one of the interpreters, "I love to feel where words come from." There is no record of the ultimate consequence of this journey, but Woolman

[19] *Ibid.*, p. 189.
[20] *Ibid.*, pp. 195–7.

had discharged his concern and left it in other hands to assess its worth.

The Scrupulous Logic of Love

There remains only to point out the scrupulous logic of love recorded in the *Journal* by which this servant of God followed down to small details the inward leadings which came to him, and to describe the closing scenes of his life.

John Woolman believed that for God there are no small things, that all that we do matters, and that, therefore, one's witness must be clear in those areas where light is given to us. Woolman, in keeping with the Quaker testimony, was a religious pacifist although in this as in other problems he saw beyond his fellows and noted that the roots of war went deeper than weapons, and that they ultimately came from our trying to get for ourselves and to keep for ourselves more than our neighbors have. Woolman would have approved of the line previously quoted from the *Imitation of Christ* which declares: "All desire peace, but they do not care for the things that pertain to true peace." He agreed with Governor Logan's shrewd argument about the inconsistency of those Philadelphia Quakers who refused to support a militia but who piled up wealth which almost invited raids from those who were not so favored. John Woolman used to link his appeals against war with the question as to whether by our accumulation of possessions we are living a life that is out of keeping with the spirit of brotherhood which must condition any enduring peace:

Oh that we who declare against wars, and acknowledge our trust in God only, may walk in the light, and therein examine our foundation and motive in holding great estates: May we look upon our treasures, and the furniture of our houses, and the garments in which we array ourselves, and try whether the seeds of war have any nourishment in these our possessions, or not.[21]

[21] Gunmere, *op. cit.*, p. 419.

Throughout the later part of his life the Woolman family dispensed with their silver service in order to trim at least this element of ostentation from their witness.

As a religious pacifist Woolman found himself in a conflict when a soldier was billeted upon him in the Indian wars in 1758. He did not refuse him since he was legally placed there, but he resolved to take no payment for it.

When the officer came to pay me, I told him I could not take pay having admitted him into my house in a passive obedience to authority. I was on horseback when he spoke to me, and as I turned from him, he said he was obliged to me; to which I said nothing; but thinking on the expression, I grew uneasy; and afterwards being near where he lived, I went and told him on what grounds I refused taking pay for the soldiers.[22]

Here is what some in the world would call a morbid scrupulosity. To Woolman it was the price of a clear witness and he did not deny that this price was not high in embarrassment and in renunciation of outward inclination.

He became deeply moved by the accounts of the conditions of slavery in the West Indies which his friend Anthony Benezet gave him. As a result he gave up the use of sugar and molasses late in his life because they were produced by such slave labor. This same feeling of longing to clear his own conduct in regard to the products of this West Indian slavery, plus some feature of the element of conformity to fashion appeared in a still more painful, because more conspicuous, form in regard to the use of dyes from the Indies which were applied to the felt or fur of men's hats to give them their conventional color. The *Journal* devotes four pages to his struggle over this matter, his desire not to affect a singularity, for he was much trusted as a man of judgment by the most responsible Quaker authorities, but his growing feeling that he must yield on this point. It

[22] *Journal*, p. 132.

concludes with the lines "when, being deeply bowed in spirit before the Lord, I was made willing to submit to what I apprehended was required of me, and when I returned home got a hat of the natural color of fur." In this as in the matter of the West Indian sweets, however, Woolman did not impose his own scruple upon his family.

When he made his final trip to England he graciously refused all offers of a gift of cabin passage and insisted upon following the "draught" in his mind toward going steerage in order better to share and know the rigors of the lives of the sailors with whom the steerage passengers were quartered.

In England in spite of his longing for communication with his family he refused to use the stagecoach post service whose cruelties to both the horses and the small boys employed by them were notorious, and Woolman sent and received letters only when Friends would carry them to the ship on their way to London.

From without, these scruples may be judged as the derangements of a neurotic mind and temperament. But seen from within they exhibit a remarkable consistency and follow a rigorous logic of love that refuses to make exceptions for oneself in order to conform to the world's expectation. Woolman's scruples were the scruples of a radical, i.e., of one who has gone to the root of things and who not only feels but acts from that root in those matters that have become clear for him.

The Final Journey

The closing scenes of his life are connected with this journey to England. By 1771, the Society of Friends in the United States, thanks to Woolman's and Benezet's tireless labors, was well on the way to having cleared its ranks of slaveholding. But Mother England was the real source of the colonial West Indian slave situation, and in 1771 the English King, George III, on behalf of British shipping interests, had ordered the governor of Virginia to put down any attempts to interfere with the slave trade. Woolman felt inwardly moved to visit England and bear his message there, and early in 1772 he was given a minute commending him to Friends in Great Britain. It was difficult to part with his family, for an ocean journey was no small undertaking in those days, but he left on May 1, 1772, from Chester, Pennsylvania, with "a feeling of the humbling hand of God upon me."

After six weeks in the squalor of steerage, he arrived in London. The London Yearly Meeting of Quakers had already begun its session, and without waiting to change his clothing, he made his way directly to this august meeting of ministers and elders and took his place among them. His coming in late and unannounced, with his hat of natural fur and his general state of dishevelment, led the dignified English Quakers to think they had a crank to deal with, and even his minute of commendation from the Friends in America and his statement that he wished only to be given liberty by that meeting to travel among English Friends with their consent did not allay this impression.

A prominent Friend arose and voiced this sentiment with the crushing suggestion that perhaps the stranger Friend might now feel his dedication of himself to this apprehended service was now accepted, and that without further labor he might now feel free to return home. Was it for this humiliating rebuff that he had left his home and work and family and made this long, difficult and hazardous journey? The tears flowed freely down Woolman's cheeks as he sat unmoved, seeking for Divine counsel before he replied. His response was characteristic of his simplicity. After some time he rose and said very simply that he did not feel himself released from the prospect of his mission in England, that of course he could not travel without their permission and that in order not to be of any expense to them, he was acquainted with a mechanical trade and that while this impediment to his service in the ministry continued he hoped that Friends would kindly employ him so that he might not be an expense to any.

After a further session of waiting, Woolman rose again and spoke from the spring of his inward ministry and with such tendering power that when he sat down the Friend who had suggested that he return home arose, confessed his error and expressed his full unity with the stranger. The meeting released Woolman for service in the ministry and he began his months of slow journeyings northward, visiting Friends and laying his concern before them on the way.

Medicine has progressed to the point in its control of disease that we have no contagious disease today that inspires a fear in any way comparable to the universal dread of the deadly smallpox that wiped out so many American communities in the eighteenth century. It had taken the life of Woolman's mother and of his eldest and most beloved sister. Many of his friends had died of it, and he could not repress his own fear that he would one day be its victim. The inoculations against it were still primitive and often themselves led to fatal infection, and Woolman had no faith in them.

John Woolman had barely arrived in the cathedral city of York where he saw a large opportunity for sharing his ministry when he fell ill of the dreaded smallpox, and in spite of the most faithful and devoted nursing by loving Friends, he died of the disease on October 7, 1772, and was buried in the meetinghouse grounds at York.

His death in the service of those he wished to free was

a fitting completion of a life that being put at God's disposal was each year brought into closer unity with those in need. The book of Ecclesiastes has a wonderful line which says "for him that is joined to all the living, there is hope." Some two and a half years before his death, John Woolman in a time of severe illness had a dream in which he saw a dull gray gloomy colored mass made up of suffering humanity and felt himself a part of it. His name was called out but he could not answer. Then a voice spoke the words, "John Woolman is dead." He took this to mean that God had extinguished something in himself and had mixed him indistinguishably with the gray mass of suffering mankind. The Quaker prayer "Lord lay on us the burden of the world's suffering" had been answered in Woolman's heart. But in this being mixed with his fellows, "joined to all the living," Woolman was also joined to the blessed Source of healing, to the inward redeemer who can minister to this suffering from within as well as from without. In his life and in his death he had become an isthmus between this healing and his fellows. And to read the *Journal* is to be lured toward this isthmus life and toward the "hope" that is promised to those who bring the needs of men and the nature of the inward redeemer together.

4

Søren Kierkegaard and
Purity of Heart

CHAPTER 4

Søren Kierkegaard and *Purity of Heart*

TO MOVE from the American John Woolman's *Journal* to the Danish Søren Kierkegaard's *Purity of Heart* is to come a century nearer to our own time, for *Purity of Heart* was written in 1846. But that does not mean that either its message or its vernacular is any nearer to our minds than John Woolman's. On the contrary, for most persons living in western Europe or America, Kierkegaard will seem like a voice from a world far-separated both in time and in temper from our own. Yet on closer acquaintance, Kierkegaard's diagnosis of our disease and the costly cure which he proposed will be seen to have been made by one who cannot be put off by any charge of having lived in a vanished world of rustic simplicity.

In a strangely universal way, Kierkegaard is both ancient and modern, both a fierce desert prophet and a metropolitan sophisticate who is all too well schooled in the artifices of modern life to be deceived by them. At any rate, to read him is to find that he has understood us well enough to have neatly blocked in advance our intended end-runs, our lateral and our forward passes, so that he has left us little choice but to plunge the center line, and there we find him advancing to tackle us and to stop us in our tracks.

Purity of Heart is an example of a brilliant devotional book that will not, however, speak to the condition of all, and that will not speak to the condition of the same man equally at different stages in his spiritual development. Like Pascal's *Thoughts*, it is a book that is ostensibly designed for the secularized man who has been enmeshed in the net of compromises that go to make up the modern worldly life. It is directed to undermine the reader's faith in the satisfying adequacy of this worldly life, although in the case of *Purity of Heart* far more than in the *Thoughts*, a static and stagnant Christianity and the static and stagnant Christian are also the object of attention. Yet in both the method is similar.

There is no leading of the man of the world by gentle steps and easy stages up to the desirability of the life of abandonment to God. Rather, both Pascal and Kierkegaard confront him continually with the most violent demands of such a life, together with blockbusting attacks that are meant to pulverize instantly the very walls of the secure dwelling in which he has lived and to turn him into a vulnerable refugee. It is as if instead of commending the new way of life by having the reader meet and be warmly drawn to such attractive exponents of it as John Woolman or Francis de Sales or Gerhard Groote, these writers took the quivering and shocked newcomer into the inner cloister of a Trappist monastery and locked him in a cell with one of the most emaciated of the silent monks kneeling at his side. But it must be confessed that not a few men have found that nothing short of this kind of shock therapy could bring them to God or could deepen their devotion.

Before setting out upon such a book, however, even if it has been written by one of such great distinction as Søren

Kierkegaard, it might be well to remember the counsel of the seventeenth-century Quaker, Isaac Penington:

He that draws another to any practice before the life in his own particular lead him, doth, as much as in him lies, destroy the soul of that person. . . . Persons are exceedingly prone to receive things as truths from those whom they have an opinion of and to imitate their practice and so hurt their own growth and endanger their own souls. . . . Let every man be fully per-suaded in his own mind. Take heed of receiving things too soon. Wait for your own particular guide and for a full persuasion of God, what is His will for you.

On Making Christianity Easy

I first came across the name Søren Kierkegaard in 1926–27 in reading Friedrich von Hügel's *Eternal Life*. The great balanced von Hügel called Søren Kierkegaard a fiercely passionate prophet of the transcendence of God, and there could hardly be any quarrel with such a designation. And yet no modern writer has been more concerned than Kierkegaard with the transcending of the transcendence, with the overcoming of the cleft between man and God, with man's abandoning himself, yielding himself to God, with man's following Christ, with the nature of the Christian's dealing with this given cleft between man and God. In fact, it is to just this issue that Kierkegaard's massive gifts as psychologist of the human soul, as philosopher, as theologian, as artist, were directed. And it is precisely this issue of yielding, of abandonment, of real faith, of commitment, that recurs most often in the whole shelf of religious literature that he wrote in less than ten years.

"How is it possible to be a Christian when one already is one," was Kierkegaard's question. Back of this lay his disillusionment with the way in which the state church tried to make Christianity easy and respectable for the ordinary citizen involved in the complexities and compromises and responsibilities of modern urban life, easy in its demands upon their worldly, comfort-centered, highly respectable lives, and easy in what it asked in the way of belief in Christian revelation by reassurances from rational argument, from the infallible authority of the Scriptures, or from the impressive historical survival of the Christian church for over eighteen centuries. Was such a diluted version which seemed bent on making only "honorary Christians"—was it really Christianity at all? And if it were, would it stand the storms that Kierkegaard's prophetic sensitivity divined were in store for it in the century ahead when its very validity would be questioned and abandoned by a large part of the so-called Christian world?

These were not theoretical problems for Kierkegaard. As the indulged son of a well-to-do manufacturer, he had entered the University of Copenhagen to study theology and had spent a decade attending its classes, living in its cultured circle, listening to its best exponents, drifting and quickening, revolting and repenting, doubting and recovering faith. At the close of this decade his father died. He had died more than once before in Kierkegaard's inward dependence upon him. Although the father was advanced in years before Søren Kierkegaard was born, he had been his son's closest friend, his image of Christian rectitude. He had died when Kierkegaard discovered the sin of the father's youth and the sin of his middle years, but each time he had come alive again. And when he died in 1838, he became "the transfigured one" the invisible companion who stood by at his prayers, who helped to draw him into his mature vocation, and who helped him conceive of what was meant by a Father's grace.

Kierkegaard found that he could not be satisfied either

by the easygoing middle-class state church standard of the Christian life which he found himself immersed in, or by the alleged obviousness of the Christian revelation. The theological lectures that he listened to which were designed to allay these misgivings, especially in regard to belief in the Christian revelation, he found unconvincing. The Hegelian rationalism that proved God's omnipresent operativeness, he found specious and if followed out he saw it dissolving away both God and the responsible individual subject in a misty immanentism, leaving no eternal encounter between man and God. He found biblical literalism being steadily undermined both by the geological and biological learning of his day and by the newer discipline of historical criticism. For the Gruntvigian arguments from history that connected the truth of the Christian revelation with its survival power in creeds and earthly institutions, he had only contempt.

And verily the eighteenth centuries . . . have not contributed an iota to prove the truth of Christianity. It is by no means true . . . that now in the nineteenth century people are far more thoroughly convinced of the truth of Christianity than they were in the first and second generations, it is rather true that just in proportion as the proof supposedly has increased in cogency . . . fewer and fewer persons are convinced.[2]

If, then, in the extremity, none of these three ways of approach can sustain belief, what should be the approach which the Christian religion offers a man who would enter into Christian truth, who would appropriate it, commit himself to it, who would become its instrument? Kierkegaard discovered increasingly the answer to this problem as he was plunged into his own existence, his own decisions

[2] *Training in Christianity* (trans. Walter Lowrie; Oxford, 1941), pp. 143-4.

and his own vocation, first by his father's death and then by an engagement with a beautiful young girl, Regine Olsen. He broke the engagement after a year and a half. The literature on the grounds for this broken engagement is voluminous: psychological unfitness for marriage due to an inherited melancholy; an attempt to shield his father's secret sin; some youthful sins of his own that conflicted with his high ideal of fitness for marriage are among the many reasons alleged for it. But more decisive than these, although none of these can be wholly excluded from consideration, would seem to have been a rising sense that he was being set apart, being singled out, being called in secret to undertake a solitary work that would consume him, and that this special calling and marriage could never be united.

Into this decision, this commitment, which no objective rational consideration could ever either confirm or deny, he plunged himself. Misunderstood, bitterly criticized, regarded as an aesthete and as a cad by Copenhagen society for his treatment of Regine, with no church or university post to give him status, he began his vocation as a writer and turned his inward suffering into an immense productivity.

From 1843–46, in addition to a most minute daily journal which he kept, he seldom published less than a book every three months and at least three of these were major works, any one of which might have satisfied an ordinary man as a magnum opus. But Kierkegaard was working under orders. He wrote for twelve hours a day. Of this period he wrote in his journal: "I have literally lived with God as one lives with a Father. Amen. I rise up in the morning and give thanks to God. Then I begin work. At a set time in the evening I break off and again give thanks to God. Then I sleep. Thus do I live." At noon when the people were at the lunch hour, he was usually seen taking his daily brief walk on the Østergade. In these years the town thought him an indulgent aesthete, living idly on his father's fortune, for most of his early writings were written under pseudonyms and were neither widely read nor widely understood. Of the personal urgency of prayer for this lonely period of his life, he could only say that if another had as much to do as he, and as little strength with which to do it, he would pray too.

Kierkegaard had always hoped that after he had written what he believed he was called to write, he might be allowed by God to retire from Copenhagen, perhaps to take a little church in the country, and to live in a more normal setting. But in 1846 at just the point when he began to think this might be possible, a literary persecution in a journal called the *Corsair* seemed to close even this door to him and to make it clear that his vocation was to stay at his post. His productivity continued in an even more mature form until 1850, and then in 1854 it quickened again in a final fiery set of polemics comparable only to Pascal's *Provincial Letters* but in Kierkegaard's case directed not against an order or a party in the church, but against the whole hypocrisy and smug lethargy of official Danish state church Christianity.

Kierkegaard and Existentialism

It is an open secret that what he has to say about commitment, about yielding, about appropriating truth, has been painfully hammered out stroke by stroke upon the anvil of his own swift life. Although his early work covered themes closely related to what we know of his own life, yet both by nature and by design he has shown not only a reticence but even a deliberate and deft concealment of the precise details of his own experience. His sufferings are tightly held between himself and God and have been used to feed the fires of his vocation as a writer. But in this furnace they have not been cast into statuesque molds which might confuse a reader into thinking that he must literally imitate them. Rather they have been consumed and have been so transmuted as to appear only in the passion and in the deep pathos and understanding with which he puts the issues to his readers.

It is as if he were to say of his own experiences and failures and triumphs: "God will hold me to account for that . . . that is God's and my problem . . . but you my reader, let us get down to what is really important. Do you live each day and each hour so that all that you are, and all that you do, and all that you plan is aware of the scrutiny and at the disposal of God?"

This way of stating the problem of commitment, of yielding, of appropriating truth, is in fact far more intensely personal than any autobiographical manner of writing could be, and yet only as this mood is understood and entered into, is it possible to feel the full thrust of such a devotional work as *Purity of Heart*. For this mood is not an accident, nor a literary cliché, but is a highly intentional vehicle of Kierkegaard's and it has behind it a whole philosophy of communication which springs out of his basic philosophy regarding the approach to the deepest levels of reality. This approach has been christened "existentialism" and has become a controversial storm center in our time.

There is no concealing the radical character of its design. For Kierkegaard insists that at all of the deeper levels where the principal problems of man's destiny have to be decided, reason of itself is impotent to tip the scales. He has only a sad pity for the conventional Rodinesque figure of man the thinker, of man head in hands in the act of deciding, of the cool impartial spectator in man's breast holding court, hearing out all of the evidence, listening carefully to accuser and accused and then from the imperturbable security of his raised dais rendering a rational verdict which our members have only to obey.

Perhaps this could not be better illustrated than by confronting this conventional impartial spectator and putting to it not mere rhetorical queries but some of the burning questions of one's own life. Shall I live as though this life is all there is? Shall I live it aesthetically as though it were a series of separate great moments in each of which I may indulge myself?

> I had a little tea-party,
>   This afternoon at three;
>   'Twas very small,
>   Three guests in all,
> Just I, myself, and me.
>
> Myself ate up the sandwiches,
>   While I drank up the tea,
>   'Twas also I
>   Who ate the pie
> And passed the cake to me.[3]

Shall I live it morally as though I were to reduce each decision to the universal principle involved, and to live as though the duties and responsibilities of my station in society, in my family, in my town, in my nation, in my profession were all that matters? Shall I live it religiously as though there were a God who is infinitely concerned for me and for the course of my life, a God who once shattered the rind of history and for a few years before his public execution revealed by his series of choices, of responses to life situations, what the character of his being and of his

---

[3] "Three Guests" by Jessica Nelson North. Used by permission.

demand on me is like? And what is the appropriate response which I should make to an encounter with such a One, to an encounter with a crucified truth that is alive and is facing me? And still further, if there should arise a conflict between these three styles of life, which one shall have the priority?

My questions would speak firmly to the impartial specta-tor. They would demand of it: "Come now, give me your verdict. You have heard out the evidence from your judicial seat. Come out of your noble equilibrium, tip the scales toward a specific decision and tell me which course I shall choose, I who have so much at stake." But I should have to add to those queries a footnote, or perhaps the principal query of all. I should have to remind the inner spectator: "Remember that in this as in every life situation your verdict alone is not enough. For I am a man and in me there are resistances and there is sin, a bent to nothingness, to dispersion as well as an aspiration to the good. There-fore if you are to help me, a man, in this critical choice, you must provide me not only with the verdict but with the holy ergs of releasing desire that can move me past dead center, past the counter drag of these resistances, or you fail me utterly in my hour of need.

"No, it is good, but in these deepest questions of all it is not enough to point out to me that each of these courses has its advantages and to enumerate them in a superbly ordered way. You have done that for me as I lay on my bed through too many nights of indecision. Nor is it enough at these levels of my being to assure me that which-ever way I choose, you will promise afterward to find me a set of the most admirable reasons for my choice. I know all too well your supple assistance in this quarter. Now, in this hour and in each subsequent hour, I must decide, I must wager my life, and my future, if there be any, on the answer that I give. It is cold comfort you give me in this extremity by your keeping on reminding me of how many things there are to consider, for I must now decide, commit, yield (for even indecision is a decision of a sort).

"Could it be, my good friend spectator, that you are not, after all, the deepest level of my being as a self? Could it be that in the critical moments of decision after your work of balanced circumspection is finished, you are suddenly called from the courtroom and forget to return? Could it be that you might even admit to me that you have been a kind of pretender to the throne of my life all along and that in all crises a long-hidden life center in me, a center that is bare of all the highly respectable official trappings of authority which the world has dressed you in, must now take over to accomplish the actual letting go and the laying hold that is all decisive? Could it be that only this hidden center could deliver me into the hands of that which could counter my bent to nothingness, to dispersion, and bring me to my true end?"

This monologue before the impartial spectator, the discursive power of reasoning in a man, may help to clarify the nature of Kierkegaard's savage attack upon it. Twenty years later Marx was to attack the objectivity of reason by insisting that the sociological, the class setting, unconsciously molds and shapes its presuppositions, and by the turn of the century, psychoanalysis and psychotherapy had challenged the objectivity of human reason on matters where the person himself was heavily involved.

Kierkegaard, however, is less of a forerunner of these movements than he is a faithful member of a company of men in whose number Tertullian, much of Augustine, Bernard of Clairvaux, Bonaventura, William of Occam, Nicholas of Cusa, and Pascal are to be found. If when it is an issue of my total life style, reason is only descriptive and is important to determine ultimate priorities, if it may even seek to deflect me from the true order of these priorities, then there must be a level in me that can encounter these priorities as they are, and that can be reached by a redeeming power that would quicken me and plunge me into accepting the real order of these dynamic priorities of my existence. And it is the task of philosophy, of psychology and of all great religious writing and preaching to seek to bare this level in a man from which the deciding, the choosing, the commiting must come. It is equally their task to use reason against itself, that is dialectically, to expose the sham evasions by which a man draws away from facing his life situation and its deepest choices. In this way these fields of study could assist in making the choice even more compelling. According to this whole school of life philosophy, however, these disciplines are neither meant, nor are they able to do more than this.

It is obvious, then, that Kierkegaard should insist that philosophy cease to exalt the study of the knowing process, epistemology, as its principal discipline and that he should belittle this whole noetic aspiration of philosophy to achieve a completely detached spectator-centered objectivity on the human situation, this attempt at an effortless contemplative mastery that would enable philosophy to reduce every concrete human decision to an example of an abstract universal principle. It is equally clear that if this point of view of Kierkegaard's be carried further it would have as little patience with philosophy's passion for ontology, the study of the ultimate nature of things, of the ultimate nature of being. Berdyaev, who freely confesses his sympathy with this school of thinkers, speaks in a similar vein of ontology in his *Spirit and Reality*, where he declares:

Metaphysics is rather apt to hypostasize concepts (i.e., to treat ideas as though they were already embodied) and then to interpret them as if they were being. The aim of ontology is to discover objective being. But it actually discovers an objectified concept. It perceives an objective being, which is the product of its own elaborated concepts. The mystery of reality is not solved by concentrating upon the object, *but by reflecting on the action of the subject.*

Kierkegaard, however, has drawn this position into focus with greater clarity than many of his predecessors by flatly denying that man's status in the universe is primarily as a speculative, reflective, life-mirroring animal. Rather, his deepest status reveals him as a divided being confronted by a series of decisions to be cast, of choices to be selected, of commitments to be made, and all of this set in an infinite cosmic frame and played within a swift span of life marked by an imminent physical death. Man for him then, is at bottom a deciding, a choosing, a self-committing animal and his destiny depends upon the manner of this exercise of that choosing, deciding, committing power in a dynamic life situation where he is being solicited from every side.

But this does not mean that all forms of choice shade into one another in a smooth continuum. On the contrary, there are sharp qualitative discontinuities which a more careful examination of the action of the subject would disclose. Kierkegaard would seem to be trying to persuade philosophy that it had missed its real goal because it had incorrectly phrased its problems, because it had put the wrong questions. By the turn he would give it, he implies that it might now come in the way of discovering a logic of subjective appropriation of truth, a logic of commitment.

Pascal has referred to these dynamic discontinuities in a significant passage toward the close of his *Thoughts* where he points to the cleft between each of the three dynamic orders and recalls that no amount of sense data can ever bridge the chasm between the senses and the intellect, and that of themselves these sense data can never compel an intellectual conclusion. And, he continues, between the order of the intellect and the order of charity there is another unbridgeable chasm. No sum of intellectual arguments can ever produce an entry into the order of charity, of loving self-yielding. For the human subject to cross these dynamic discontinuities requires a change of mode, a giving up of the mode of the one and an entry into the mode of the other.[4]

It was, then, upon this process of yielding, of making the leap, of moving from one intensity of living, from one dynamic mode of choice of appropriation of truth to another, that Kierkegaard wishes to refocus philosophy and theology and all religious writing and preaching. His own brilliant distinction of the three orders or levels or intensities of choice involved in the aesthetic, the moral and the religious "Stages on Life's Way" were only exercises in this kind of recasting of philosophy's problem.

The radical nature of what this approach asks philosophy and religious discourse to do can be compared to an editor demanding a writer to recast his article substituting active verbs for all static nouns. For example, if philosophy were to recast its dealing with physical death and immortality after this demand, it would mean a giving up of any attempt to define the self as an enduring substance or related to an enduring substance by which means metaphysicians have ordinarily sought to establish the self's persistence in death. Instead, philosophy would be compelled to go about examining the nature of the human situation, and to see what dynamic capacity in the self this act of abandonment in-

[4] Blaise Pascal, *Thoughts* (Everyman ed.; New York: E. P. Dutton & Co., Inc.), pp. 234–5.

volved in death really exposed, and then to go about searching life for other evidence of the nature and significance of this mode of yielding.

Although this is not the place to discuss the matter, there is no desire to hide the enormous difficulties which such an understanding must encounter, or the ghastly dangers involved where the new dynamism, the almost exclusive focus upon the intensity of the commitment, without any substantive norms, may plunge into daemonism or nihilism. To Kierkegaard and the Christian company to which he belonged, the method was always used within a Christian frame and as an auxiliary discipline to quicken men into the choice of the deepest priority within this Christian frame. And there is some evidence to indicate that while Kierkegaard, like his predecessors, insisted that he, too, was just a pilgrim, and that he dared to give some elementary instructions on pilgrimaging only because he had himself been so long on the road and had had so many accidents along the way, in truth he knew at first hand more of the character of the shrine which the pilgrimage meant to reach than his exclusive discussion of the activity of the journeying itself would lead one to believe.

Neither Kierkegaard nor those moved by him to attempt this radical re-examination of philosophy's problems have been able to carry through so drastic a reorientation with full consistency. There are always lapses from verbs into nouns again. Even the most radical impressionistic painter either fortunately or unfortunately cannot cleanse his art of all photographic elements in his attempt to focus exclusively upon his own inward response to the scene. Nevertheless this is the existential mood that fired Kierkegaard as he tore out of himself book after book to give it expression, and this is the mood that penetrates each page of his *Purity of Heart*.

Existentialism and Kierkegaard's Method

It is a mood that determines his method. He will lay bare the will. He will expose that level in man from which the yielding, the committing, the abandoning comes. In every man there is an "infinite abyss that can only be filled by an infinite and immutable object, that is to say, only by God himself," declares Pascal.[5] Kierkegaard will scrape away the coatings that have formed over this abyss in man; the lures of the world, the deceitful rationalizations of the divided self, the capacity to escape judgment by comparing oneself with others, by hiding in the crowd. This method of peeling, of stripping, of exposing, of unmasking, is only sadistically cruel to one who would cling tightly to his illusions, to his mass neurosis, to his insincerity, to his humbug, perhaps to his attempt to go on dabbling with, playing at Christianity. "For God," observes Kierkegaard, "can have nothing to do with an insincere man." He tells a story of a leper named Simeon who sat among the tombs, an outcast from the community because of his sores. Then he found an ointment that would drive his sores inward and make them invisible and by this deception enable him to be pronounced well by the priest and once more able to mingle with his fellows, although he would still infect them. Should he use the ointment or reject it? For Kierkegaard, there are times when it is not only a kindness but the deepest mercy to be cruel. For gentle treatment in such an exigency may encourage the use of the salve, set the reader at ease too soon—to his ultimate destruction. "Do not for God's sake, repair to anyone to be set at ease," he warns.[6]

This method may be seen, on the other hand, to be one that respects deeply the freedom of each human being, the

[5] *Ibid.*, p. 113.
[6] *Training in Christianity*, p. 69.

freedom to perish quite as well as the freedom to commit himself to the highest. Back of every line that he wrote in *Purity of Heart* breathes Kierkegaard's own deep personal conviction that "a pure heart is first and last a bound heart —bound to God." [7] Yet if commitment, if the binding of a living being to a living truth is a lifelong series of acts of willing, of yielding, of self-donation, then obviously these must be freely undertaken or freely rejected by the subject himself. And there is no objective way, no outward method of passing over this condition of commitment from one person or one group of persons to another. In spite of the habitual inclinations induced by outer religious symbols or practices, in spite of the impressiveness of an array of rationally compelling proofs, neither of these can fully communicate Christian commitment to another person. Such commitment is an act which a subject must himself in the depths of his own heart face and decide.

Thus Kierkegaard would suit the method of the religious address to the occasion. It must take its readers to the infinite abyss in themselves and to the infinite and immutable pursuer who alone can fill that abyss, and it must leave them there. It must reveal what commitment is, what it involves, what it costs, in what ways men flee from it, and what follows on such abandonment. It must describe what commitment meets with in the majesty of God, in the forgiveness of God, the grace of God, in the unchangeable constancy of God, in the promises of Christ, in the initiative of the Eternal. It must confront men with a choice. But the very nature of its choice being personal and a matter that must emerge from a personal subject, it cannot go further. What a drastic revision in the average sermon would be necessitated if this method were to be widely adopted.

[7] *Collected Works* (Danish ed.) ; IX, 142.

How to Listen to a Devotional Address

A good place to begin reading *Purity of Heart* is well along toward the end where Kierkegaard talks of the listener's role in a devotional address. For here Kierkegaard, in keeping with the existential method of approach, would produce a situation where the listener might be aroused to his true situation and placed before a decision.

The average Protestant who comes to listen to a devotional address or to a sermon, comes to be edified. He seats himself and feels that he has done his share in coming to the place of worship, and that now it is up to the speaker to do his part. He is prepared to listen to the speaker much as he is prepared to listen to a lecture at a public forum or to watch the performance of an actor on the stage. In this mood he reserves the right to pass judgment both upon the content of the message and upon the artistry of the performance.

Kierkegaard drew upon the old Danish stage of the early nineteenth century for his analogy, and insisted that if the reader is to learn to listen properly to a devotional address or a sermon, he must be prepared for a drastic reorientation that will jar him out of the passive, auditor role he has been permitted to sink into. Instead of the speaker of the address or sermon being the actor on the stage and the listener being the audience, Kierkegaard insists that the listener take his place as the sole actor upon the stage. The passive listener thus suddenly becomes the actor. And the audience is now, not his fellow listeners. No, his audience is a single One who patiently and quietly waits for him to begin going through his part. The silent, patient auditor is God. And the speaker, whom the listener has ordinarily expected to take the role of actor, where is he now? In this change of roles, the speaker now becomes the prompter. As such, he is like the prompter hidden in the wings of the old Danish theater who spoke over softly the actor's lines so that in case the actor wandered, he could by this prompting recover his true course again. Now the true listener to the devotional address is given the decisive role of examining his actions before the gaze of God, with the speaker and the content of the address merely serving to prompt him on some of the areas that he may have neglected.

There is no attempt here to remove responsibility from the speaker and lay it all upon the listener. The preacher, too, is under divine scrutiny and is responsible to God both in what he says and for what he is, that he may not stand between the listener and his decisive role of standing singled out and open before God. He must not stand in the listener's light but he must take him to the light. The pulpit of the devotional address is, therefore, always at the side, always in the wings and never in the center.

The devotional address *Purity of Heart* is itself a part of a longer volume entitled *Edifying Addresses of Varied Tenor* that was written in 1846 as Kierkegaard had finished what he believed to be his principal religious and philosophical task, and was published the following year. It represents one of his most mature pieces of writing. Professor Geismar, who devoted much of his life to a study of Kierkegaard, says of it, "It seems to me that nothing he has written has sprung so directly out of his relationship with God as this address. Anyone who wishes to understand Kierkegaard properly will do well to begin with it." [8]

"A Pure Heart Is First and Last a Bound Heart"

This address is a long meditation on the sentence, "Purity of heart is to will one thing," based upon a verse from the Epistle of James: "Draw nigh to God, and he will draw nigh

[8] E. Geismar, *Søren Kierkegaard* (German ed.; 1929), p. 490.

to you. Cleanse your hands, ye sinners; and purify your hearts, ye double minded" (4:8). The occasion for this meditation on purity of heart as the willing of one thing was as a preparation for the time of confession in the liturgy of the Lutheran church. But there is no further reference to the specific catechism of the liturgy, and readers of all denominations or of none are led at once to consider the whole meaning and purpose of an occasion of confession to God.

The assumption at the outset is that the one confessing wants to restore a truth relationship between his own consciousness and God, wants to recover "purity of heart." There is no suggestion that by confession, God's knowledge of the one confessing is increased.

Not God, but you, the maker of the confession, get to know something by your act of confession. Much that you are able to keep hidden in darkness, you first get to know by your opening it to the knowledge of the all-knowing One. Even the most atrocious misdeeds are committed, even blood is spilt, and many times it must in truth be said of the guilty one: he knew not what he did. . . . For does passion ever properly know what it does? [9]

One may make this act of confession in company with others, but in the deepest sense one can only make it as an individual, alone before God. And the confession must ask how he has lived as an individual. The purpose of the devotional address upon this occasion is only to separate out, to individualize, to prompt, to put questions, to cover the probable ground of the difficulties.

Nicholas of Cusa, in the middle of the fifteenth century, stopped to visit the monks at Terstegen in the course of his arduous journey of reform as papal legate to the churches of

[9] *Purity of Heart*, p. 23.

Germany and the Low Countries, and these monks extracted from him a promise to write them a set of exercises or meditations that would help them prepare themselves inwardly for the vision of God about which he had preached to them. When he fulfilled his promise to them sometime later, he sent the study to them together with a painting which they were to put up in their chapel. The painting showed simply the all-seeing eye of God. It was so executed, however, that no matter at what angle one looked at it, the eye seemed to be focused singly and lone upon the beholder. The treatise was called *De Visione Dei, The Gaze of God,* and the picture served to illuminate and focus almost every page of the writing.

Not many writers have been so shrewd as to furnish such a visual key to what they have to say, but it has often occurred to me that almost every really creative author has one or two master images that hover in his own unconscious life and profoundly influence all that he writes. If these could be discovered there is perhaps nothing that would so readily yield an inside grasp of what he longs to communicate. Yet, alas, these master images too seldom appear as frontispieces. In Kierkegaard's *Journals,* however, he mentions more than once a scene that haunted him. It was a memory of walks he had taken on the Jutland heath. Here where there are no trees and where the vegetation is so dwarfed and sparse, he remembered that try as he would a man could not conceal himself from another's view. And the memory of Adam's futile attempt to hide himself from God's view after his sin, settled over this image and carried it beyond the casual return drift of remembered experience for him. I believe that this image furnished him with a kind of precipitating power for a host of thoughts about the relationship of man to God upon the occasion of confession and that to be aware of it is to possess a kind of philosopher's stone, a miraculous substance that can re-distill his original mood and illuminate almost every turn of the discourse of *Purity of Heart*.

The meditation seeks to help the reader out of human swarms of the city, out of the well-cultivated and populated farm land of the city's hinterland where there are still human shelters to hide in, and out onto the open heath where he may no longer escape scrutiny and where the act of confession will enable him to know himself as he is known by the Eternal. The Negro spiritual, "There's No Hidin' Place Up There" sings of the true condition of this time of confession. For only as the reader can be stripped clean, may he know what he most deeply wills and whether it is really one thing or many conflicting things. And only by this return to such scrutiny under the quiet gaze of the Eternal can the purity of heart, the purity of single-minded-ness, be restored. Only so can the worldly *double-minded-ness* that corrodes every man who is not so renewed, only so can it be faced, acknowledged, forgiven, and dissolved away.

The Role of Memory in Confession

For Kierkegaard, in *Purity of Heart,* there are certain human faculties, human capacities which will serve to help the man who sincerely seeks to confess. One of these is memory. For it is memory that has a way of visiting double-minded persons and recasting the scene of their past in a way that may cause them great pain.

Now memory also visits the double-minded person. Then it says to him, "Do you remember that time? . . . You as well as I knew well enough what was there required of you, but you shrank back (to your own destruction), do you remember that! It was by this that you won a great deal of your property (to your own destruction). Do you remember that! Do you recall that time?"

. . . But the popular one says, "Only keep quiet, never let any-one get to know it." "Very well," memory answers. "You know that I am no petty bickerer who is in desperation over what is owed him. Let it rest. No one shall get to know it, as long as you live, perhaps not even when you are dead and forgotten. But eternally, eternally it will continue to be remembered." [10]

Yet Kierkegaard is as ready to reveal the blessed comfort of memory to one who has taken the "Northerne Passage" to which he was called, to one who has drunk the cup and said yes to the light. There are few passages in literature that present this solace of remembered decision more appealingly. He is speaking of one who wills one thing:

He becomes a friend, a lover of memory. And so when in a quiet hour, memory visits him (and already at this point how different it is from that visit when memory threateningly knocks at the door of the double-minded man!), then it says to him, "Do you remember that time, that time when the good resolution conquered within you?" And he answers, "Yes, dear one!" But then memory continues . . . "Can you remember all the hardships and sufferings you endured for the sake of the resolution?" He answers, "No, dear one, I have forgotten that—let it remain forgotten! But when in the toils of life and struggle, when in my troubled thoughts all is in confusion, it may seem to me as if even that was forgotten which I know I had willed in sincerity. Oh, thou hast thy very name from that act of remembering, thou messenger of the Eternal: Memory. At that hour, visit me, and bring with thee the long-desired, the strengthening meeting with thyself once more." And memory answers in parting, "I promise you that, I swear it to you by all eternity." [11]

To the single-minded man, this welcome guest of memory "is his reward and this reward is above all others."

[10] *Ibid.*, pp. 110, 113.
[11] *Ibid.*, pp. 121–2.

Remorse and Seasoned Repentance

But memory only reopens the scenes of past performance in confession. It is only the agent of a deeper inner activity which it is yet within the confessing man's will to give or to withhold. That deeper level of activity is remorse and repentance. Remorse, however, has two levels that interpenetrate each other. On the one hand, remorse is the review in memory of an act which recovers the fluid moment in the will when the direction of that act hung in the balance between several courses. This level of remorse includes the realization that the act could have been other than it was, and it is an eloquent witness to the freedom of the human spirit that such a review is possible.

But there is a second level of remorse. This level, looking in memory at this fluid moment, is acutely aware of the right course that should have been taken and was not, and is accompanied by a sense of guilt and a feeling of grief that the right way was rejected and the wrong way taken. This second level is a witness to more than the freedom of the human spirit. It is a witness to the fact that the "little liberty" of the human spirit, its freedom, is given to man to spend in the purchase of the "greater liberty" of single-mindedly willing the good, and that when this is not done, the agony of the spirit's frustration of its true function makes itself felt by the grief and pain of the guilt that marks remorse.

Repentance is a possible but not inevitable further stage of remorse. When there comes not only a realization of failure, not only a burst of contrition for having failed the good, not only a readiness to admit this failure freely to oneself and others with whatever humbling blow to the obesity of the ego this may involve, but also a determination not to fail the good again, a rekindling of ardor for the good and a resolve to turn around and be swift in its service—this is repentance.

Now, for Kierkegaard this measured remorse and repentance is the heart of what true confession should accomplish, and his invitations to it are moving. Remorse, according to Kierkegaard, is a guide given man by Providence for his salvation.

He [Remorse] is not so quick of foot as the indulgent imagination, which is the servant of desire. He is not so strongly built as the victorious intention. He comes on slowly afterwards. He grieves. But he is a sincere and faithful friend. If that guide's voice is never heard, then it is just because one is wandering along the way of perdition. . . . So wonderful a power is remorse, so sincere is its friendship that to escape it entirely is the most terrible thing of all.[12]

True remorse precipitates decision once again and decision is always made *now,* made in the *eleventh hour,* made beyond postponement and delay, and Kierkegaard makes much of this focusing of past and future time on the critical moment in confession—on the *now* in order that this moment may yield fruit.

When remorse awakens concern, whether it be in the youth, or in the old man, it awakens it always at the eleventh hour. . . . It is not deceived by a false notion of a long life, for it is the eleventh hour. . . . He who repents at any other hour of the day repents in the temporal sense. He fortifies himself by a false and hasty conception of the insignificance of his guilt. He braces himself with a false and hasty notion of life's length. His remorse is not in true inwardness of spirit. Oh, eleventh hour, wherever thou art present, how all is changed! [13]

But the "eleventh hour," the need to decide, to yield, the realization that the thousand-mile journey begins with

12 *Ibid.,* pp. 9–10.
13 *Ibid.,* pp. 12–13.

a single step has no intention of pressing a headlong and precipitate repentance. Kierkegaard's logic of passion is far too discerning to be deceived by dramatic great moments, by impulsive paroxysms of either grief or ecstasy. He is not inviting his readers to a kind of holy epilepsy. He knows too well that after the convulsive ecstatic fit is over, the patient has not moved up to a sounder state of health. "Sudden repentance would drink down all the bitterness of sorrow in a single draught and then hurry on. It wants to get away from guilt. . . . But impatience, no matter how long it rages, never becomes repentance." [14]

True repentance, then, is not only deliberate but it endures. This insight seems to have been refined and tempered in the slow fire of Kierkegaard's own life experience. The grief of true repentance is not something that passes away when once realized and faced. Rather this grief remains with the sinner always and even deepens the older it gets and the more a man commits himself to the Eternal.

This may seem to be a morbid, masochistic clutching of grief for grief's sake. But on deeper consideration its profound insight reveals itself. For while fully forgiven, these failures serve to remind him of how much he has been forgiven and of how much he has failed that which he loved. And the deeper the love, the more the awareness of failure. A saint who feels the weight of his early sins (sins that in the world's judgment are of little consequence) is not on that account a melancholy neurotic. It is in the light of the passion of his great love that those early failures which cling always to him grow in their weight. But they come to be weights which he carries to his salvation, no matter how heavy they may seem, for they draw him into his true relationship with the forgiving Other after whom he has flung his life. Kierkegaard adds:

[14] *Ibid.*, pp. 16, 15.

It is not a gain that guilt should be wholly forgotten. On the contrary, it is loss and perdition. But it is a gain to win an inner intensity of heart through a deeper and deeper inner sorrowing over guilt. . . . It is a gain to notice that a man has grown older by the deeper and deeper penetration into his heart of the transformation wrought by remorse. . . . When punishment . . . becomes a blessing, when consequences even become redemptive. . . . This is the older, the strong and the powerful repentance.[15]

Confession and the Abyss

The ultimate service of memory, remorse and repentance in confession, however, is to bring men to the brink of the existential abyss of commitment again. In the inner rhythm of the liturgy of the church, it is not by chance that the act of confession is followed by the taking of the sacrament with the renewed act of consecration and commitment involved. But before this consecration and commitment can be really earnest, before a man dare pray the fifteenth-century Swiss prayer, "Strip me, oh God, of all that separates me from Thee, and give me that which will unite me to Thee. Strip me of myself and give me Thyself"—before this can be more than sonorous reverie-filled words drifting across the lips, there must be a realization of need, an exposure of one's true condition that wrings such a prayer from trembling lips. It is this which a true act of confession, according to Kierkegaard, is trying to accomplish.

Carlyle, in *Sartor Resartus*, pleasantly suggests that there has always been an unuttered query in his mind as to whether the pompous silk and broadcloth bishops who strut about in the House of Lords could strike such poses if they were naked, and Kierkegaard in his *Works of Love* asks the reader to imagine in the enchanted world of the theater that one night the players got confused and believed that

[15] *Ibid.*, pp. 17–18.

they actually *were* the characters they represented, and then to recall that in the course of life men also get confused in this way and think that they actually are what the world says that they are. Continuing his role of prompter, Kierkegaard in his deliberate and exhaustive way describes to the listener-actor, to the confused listener-actor who is perhaps unconscious that he is confused about his role, some of the symptoms of double-mindedness, of mistaking the worldly costume for the real man that he is. These symptoms have a way of showing him how far he is from being all of one piece, from being single of eye, pure of heart, from willing one thing—the only thing that is one thing, from willing the Good, from possessing "a bound heart—bound to God."

In this pathology of double-mindedness, Kierkegaard describes men in pursuit of honor, of black inches in a *Who's Who* insertion, of "fruit salad" over a soldier's heart, of the seats at the world hostess' right and left, and of how they must tack and trim sail to come by them. To will honor is not to will *one* thing. He shows the pleasure seeker led to despair in spite of his skillful rotation of crops and left ever longing for more. To will pleasure is not to will one thing. He describes a man seeking rewards, seeking to avoid punishment, seeking to serve the Good only if it can be obvious that if the Good wins it will owe its victory to him. He shows men willing the Good to a certain extent. He shows them plunging into busyness, into distractions, and then clutching violently at comparisons between themselves and the mass of men in order to show that they are no worse than others, that their credit still holds, that they still have money in the bank of public esteem.

Alone Before the Eternal

But Kierkegaard's existential armory has more than one weapon for loosening the actor-listener's stage costume and bringing him to himself. In addition to the convicting diagnosis of double-mindedness that he so adeptly supplies, *Purity of Heart* is full of reminders of the Eternal auditor before whom the listener-actor examines himself in the devotional address.

Francis de Sales' first instruction in prayer, "Remember into whose presence you come" is here elaborated, and the listener is made freshly aware of the individuating and searching gaze of the Eternal One from whom nothing is hidden and to whom all secrets are known. The Jutland heath appears again as Kierkegaard describes the soul's condition of utter transparency before God, before the Eternal. There is no hiding in the crowd here, no flattening out behind a clump of comparisons, no raising of the screen of the regard in which the world holds one. In eternity and before the Eternal

he shall be brought to account strictly as an individual. . . . For, after all, what is eternity's accounting other than that the voice of conscience is forever installed with its eternal right to be the exclusive voice? What is it other than that throughout eternity an infinite stillness reigns wherein the conscience may talk with the individual. . . . It must be heard. There is no place to flee from it. For in the infinite there is no place, the individual is himself the place. It must be heard. In vain the individual looks about for the crowd. Alas, it is as if there were a world between him and the nearest individual, whose conscience is also speaking to him about what *he* as an individual has spoken, and done, and thought of good and of evil.[16]

"Eternity . . . never counts. . . . The sober countenance of eternity quietly waits." In his *Works of Love* Kierkegaard writes:

Oh that I might show the face of Eternity when the rich man in reply to the question as to whether he had been merciful

[16] *Ibid.*, pp. 169–170.

answers, "I have given away a hundred thousand dollars to the poor!" For eternity will look at him surprised as one who cannot get it into his head what the rich man is talking about; and then eternity will again propound the question, "Have you been merciful?" Imagine a man who went out to a mountain to talk with it about his affairs; or that a man had dealings with the wind about his own achievements: eternity will no more understand what the rich man is talking about concerning the hundred thousand and what the powerful men mean by saying that they have done everything, than the mountain or the wind understood what was said to them. . . . Is it compassionate to give hundreds of thousands to the poor? No. Is it compassionate to give half a shilling to the poor? No. Compassion depends on: how it is given . . . . Still let us not forget that compassion may be shown in both instances.[17] [For] eternity never counts. The sober countenance of eternity quietly waits. And if all the generations that have lived on earth rose up and gathered themselves in a single crowd in order to loose a storm against eternity, in order to coerce eternity by their colossal majority: eternity would scatter them as easily as the firmness of an immovable rock would scatter the frothy scum; as easily as the wind when it rushes forward scatters chaff. . . . eternity scatters the crowd by giving each an infinite weight, by making him heavy—as an individual.[18]

But here as always, this existential notion of eternity is not in terms of a place, but of a condition. With Nathan Söderblom, *Purity of Heart* might have said, "Now is eternity." Kierkegaard continues:

In eternity there are chambers enough so that each may be placed alone in one. For wherever conscience is present, and it is and shall be present in each person, there exists in eternity a lonely prison, or the blessed chamber of salvation. On that account this consciousness of being an individual is the primary

[17] *Collected Works* (Danish ed.) , IX, pp. 311–12.
[18] *Purity of Heart*, p. 177.

consciousness in a man, which is his eternal consciousness. . . .
My listeners, do you at present live in such a way that you are
yourself clearly and eternally conscious of being an individual? [19]

After an hour's vigil under the rays of this deliberate light,
any listener-actor who finds that he has nothing to confess,
nothing to repent, and no longing to commit himself afresh
to the Source of the Good will be either already in an en-
viable stage of blessedness or in a state that is opaque to
the normal forms of penetration.

The Figure of the Incurable Sufferer

But these have been direct descriptions of the symptoms
of double-mindedness and of the One whom the double-
minded one confronts. When Jesus found that even his
disciples seemed more concerned about which of them
should be first in the kingdom than in what he was trying
to teach them about abandonment to the service of God,
Kierkegaard notes that he placed a little child in the midst
of them that it might recall them to their true condition.
Instead of a child, Kierkegaard places a sufferer among his
double-minded listener-actors. But it is not an ordinary
sufferer who may sooner or later expect to be well again.
Rather it is an Incurable Sufferer who is selected for this
mission. It is a sufferer for whom there is utterly no hope
in this world, one who is and must remain until his in-
definitely postponed death, wholly and completely a care
to others, one who cannot wrench away from the abyss and
drug himself with expectations that although he is busy
today, tomorrow he will serve the good in double measure:
as soon as he has acquired a material competency, as soon
as he has finished this big job, painted this great picture,
fought this one more war, reached the age of retirement.

[19] *Ibid.*, pp. 177–9.

The Incurable Sufferer, in fact, can never actively serve the Good at all, never. Here in this figure Kierkegaard lays bare the very nub of religious commitment. At its deepest level—and true religion is not to be found on any other —it is all or none. Thomas Huxley once remarked that it does not take much of a man to make a Christian, but it takes all there is of him. Suppose that *you* should become the Incurable Sufferer. Do you know a level of yielding that would make even such an existence of infinite meaning? Can even an Incurable Sufferer will one thing, do all, give all, suffer all for the Good? The answers that the listener-actor gives to these questions are self-revealing. When Eckhart says that the kingdom of heaven is only for the perfectly dead, he is trying to express the same thought. But the "perfectly dead" are not dead in the sense, for example, of Charles Morgan's neo-stoical aspiration for invulnerability, for the power to be able to stand anything. What Kierkegaard and Eckhart mean is precisely the opposite. To be "perfectly dead" is to have become infinitely vulnerable, infinitely woundable. It is to let go and to hold on, to live from moment to moment from a source of strength that is sufficient but not self-sufficient. It is to let go the self-sufficiency and to lay hold of One who shrouds both what He will ask of a man and the strength, or almost better expressed, the weakness which he will be given to fulfill it. "Though I walk through the valley . . . Thou . . . Thy rod and Thy staff . . ."

With commitment, Kierkegaard's existential message begins and ends. With it he labors through every volume, and in none more directly or more passionately than in *Purity of Heart*. Here in the presence of his moving figure of the Incurable Sufferer it is as if someone should look long and knowingly into our eyes and ask, "When you pray the Lord's prayer, do you really dare to add, 'Thy will be done

—in me'? Not, Thy will be done to a certain extent; not, Thy will be done so long as it is in keeping with the natural aspirations and human expectations of a man; not, Thy will be done so long as I never become the Incurable Sufferer; but 'Thy will be done—in me'?"

Vocation and the Final Question

But as one stands before such a burning question, can he be forgiven if he dares to ask what the commitment implied may mean for his present responsibilities, for his vocation? For Kierkegaard this is a matter of qualitative priorities. Whose will is first? Are you ready for all and have you cast your faith upon Him who is sufficient for all? It is no mechanical question of all men giving up the work they are doing and doing something else. But it may change your status or it may confirm you in it.

No, it is a question of whether in each thing that you do

you are conscious of your eternal responsibility before God. Do you live in such a way that this consciousness is able to secure the time and quiet and liberty of action to penetrate every relation of your life? This does not demand that you withdraw from life, from an honorable calling, from a happy domestic life. On the contrary, it is precisely that consciousness which will sustain and clarify and illuminate what you are to do in the relations of life. You should not withdraw and sit brooding over your eternal accounting. To do this is to deserve something further to account for.[20]

In other words, what will be asked of you will be shown you. But only a step at a time.

It can sometimes demand that a man leave his esteemed calling and put on lowliness, that he give away all his possessions to the poor, that he shall not even dare to bury his father. Again

[20] *Ibid.*, pp. 181–2.

it can demand of others that they shall assume the power and the dignity that are offered them, that they shall take over the working power of wealth, that they shall bury the father, and that perhaps a large part of their lives shall be consecrated to faithfulness which is to be faithful over the little to this extent, that their own life has no claims of its own, but rather is faithful to the memory of the departed one.[21]

In short, the matter of vocation or life-setting is again resolved into a question of commitment.

Kierkegaard wrote:

To live in the religious spirit is not easy; the believer is continually on a deep sea 70,000 fathoms deep. . . . It is a *great* thing floating on 70,000 fathoms of water and beyond all human aid to be happy: it is a little thing and not at all religious to swim in shallow water with a host of waders. . . . No matter how long the religious man lies out there, it does not mean that little by little he will reach land again. He can become quieter, attain a sense of security, love jests and the merry mind. But to the last moment, he lies over 70,000 fathoms of water.[22]

Christina Rossetti says it all in four lucid lines:

> Will the road wind uphill all the way?
> Yes, to the very end.
> Will the journey take the whole long day?
> From dawn to dusk, my friend.

The image of the Incurable Sufferer, then, is a threat, an unfrocking, a stripping that asks us where we are in commitment. If "a pure heart is first and last a bound heart—bound to God" and if God took all, if he took even my power of intellect, "then all I have left to be inspired by is . . . 'my relation to God' which can well survive, yes

---

[21] *Ibid.*, p. 101.
[22] *Stages on Life's Way* (Danish ed.) , VI, p. 414.

probably become even more intense if he took this gift away from me. The whole art lies in being inspired, in being glad over 70,000 fathoms of water" for thine is the kingdom, and the power and the glory—the glory forever.

One day in October, 1855, Søren Kierkegaard collapsed on the street in Copenhagen and was taken to the hospital. In a few weeks he died. He was forty-two years of age. He had tried to be faithful to his vocation although he knew that his peculiar life style as a writer was his own and not another's. He believed that he had been singled out for his task. He was born and he lived and he died *hiin enkelte,* that solitary individual. But from a final conversation with his friend Boeson in the hospital just before his death, we know that he died in perfect peace and confidence in the amplitude of the Grace that was sufficient even for him. He always denied that he was a Christian in the highest sense. But he had tried to fulfill his calling to enunciate what that Christianity was and what it required. He had not tried to make Christianity easy, but he had tried to stab it awake. His message would scarcely be more effectively gathered up than in the words of his Spanish disciple, Unamuno, when he declares in the closing lines of his *Tragic Sense of Life:* "God deny you peace, and give you glory."

5

The *Selected Letters* of *Friedrich von Hügel*

CHAPTER 5

The *Selected Letters* of Friedrich von Hügel

NEXT TO a face to face visit with a friend, there is probably no form of communication that is so satisfying as a good letter. For a good letter is intimate and personal and has cost a period of caring and of opening the heart and mind when it was written, and it is likely to arouse a similar opening on the part of the one who receives it. When the letters are between mature friends who share not alone the assurances of mutual affection but their best thoughts and counsel with each other, the correspondence may equal and occasionally even surpass in value the personal visit. For judgment and wisdom are often encouraged by the quiet, cool impartiality under which the letter is written and just as the screen in the confessional preserves a semblance of privacy between the kneeling one and the spiritual counselor which may make it easier for each to pour out to the other what is right, so the distance present between the writer and the receiver may nerve the writer to say clearly and simply what might be far less easy for him to express and for the other to receive were they seated together in a free conversation. Conversations, furthermore, cannot be recalled as carefully and accurately as these written visits and they can only rarely be recovered sufficiently to share them with others.

When, therefore, some great mind and soul has poured out the best of his thought in an exchange of insights or in counsel or in spiritual direction in the form of letters, not only are the immediate receivers favored, but ultimately others may share in the measured counsel and wisdom which they contain. The interest in such spiritually seasoned letters is very old in the Christian tradition and apart from those which were included in the Canon of Scripture itself, the letters of Jerome, Bernard of Clairvaux, Theresa of Ávila, Francis de Sales, Fénelon, Caussade, Forbes-Robinson, Paul Claudel, John Chapman, and of Evelyn Underhill have been a part of the spiritual staple on which countless Christian seekers have been fed. The *Selected Letters* of Friedrich von Hügel belong in this company of devotional literature, and since their publication in 1927, two years after Baron von Hügel's death, they have been highly prized by an ever-growing group of discriminating readers both in England and the United States, who have found in them a rare combination of stimulus for the mind, and of nurture for the soul.

Living his adult life in England, Baron Friedrich von Hügel was that vanishing phenomenon in the Anglo-Saxon world of letters, a *privat-Gelehrte,* a scholar who was not dependent upon a professional university post or an ecclesiastical or public station for his living, but who gave himself with abandon to the fields of his choice. For this reason, he may have had more time to give to friends or to those who sought out his help than do most of those who are caught up in the bustle of public duties or of earning a living. But after an early attack of typhus, his health was so frail that for much of his life he could not give more than from three to four hours a day to writing, so that his letters were always written out of a slender capital of time and energy and at no small cost to the time he was carefully shepherding for his important scholarly works.

His daughter, Baroness Hildegard von Hügel wrote of her father's generous giving of himself both in receiving personal visits and in the countless letters that he was always writing:

He was the most faithful friend. In spite of his health which had always curtailed his energies, he never would let it interfere when it came to giving sympathy and interest to people who wrote to him in distress or came to him as they did from all over the world, for help and advice. I used sometimes to begrudge the labour and pains he took in answering some very trivial and superficial person who wrote to him long pages of doubts, etc. but to whom he gave his whole mind and failing strength to advise, to stimulate, to greater faith, more perseverance, etc.[1]

I have copies of two unpublished letters which Baron von Hügel wrote to a Swedish Quaker woman whom I know in answer to her telling him about a religious experience of her own. Each is three single-spaced typewritten pages long and deals with her problem with the most amazing discernment.

The Baron's niece, Gwendolyn Green, in a little-known memoir called *Two Witnesses* describes the life out of which these letters came:

From the first, he had to accept ill health that kept him like a prisoner; and deafness [from the typhus] that though he never spoke of it, must have held him back from many things. . . . He lived in a deep interior world—where few, perhaps can follow— giving himself an interior life; tearing as it were, out of himself great chunks of truth and bringing them to the surface.[2]

[1] *Selected Letters*, p. 67.
[2] Gwendolyn Green, *Two Witnesses* (New York: E. P. Dutton & Co., Inc., 1930) , p. 101.

Due to his deafness, conversations with von Hügel were of necessity mainly monologues. Because of this, the characterization of visits with von Hügel by Canon Lilley, one of the Baron's most devoted friends, is perhaps applicable to his correspondence as well.

They seemed to have divined beforehand, and now to have the one purpose of satisfying, your special need of the moment, a need of which perhaps you had never been fully aware until that moment, but which under the spell of that eager abundance of exposition had become for the moment your whole and sole self. In that high debate the talker seemed to exist for the sake of the listener and the latter knew, or he was not worthy to be there, that it was a momentous hour. The encyclopaedic knowledge, the rich profound stores of wisdom, were being outpoured for his sake. He was being guided, sustained, invigorated in and by that great flood of speech. . . . But the brilliant talker was really a silent man. He lived most vividly, most satisfyingly, in meditation; and out of that prolonged meditation upon the deepest things of the spirit were formed those pearls of spiritual wisdom which he afterwards strung upon a thread of purest gold.[3]

The Making of a European Christian Mind

What was the life and career and point of view out of which these letters were quarried? There was scarcely a principal country in Europe outside of Spain that did not have some share in forming Friedrich von Hügel's personality. His father, Baron Carl, was descended from an old noble Rhineland family. At an early age, he had, after the example of his own father, entered the service of the Austrian government as a military officer. This was followed by extensive travels and naturalistic expeditions in the Orient following his own scientific interests, further military

[3] Maude Petre, *Von Hügel and Tyrrell* (New York: E. P. Dutton & Co., Inc., 1938), pp. viii-x.

service, and, in 1850, appointment as Austrian Minister to the Grand Ducal State of Tuscany. It was here in his middle fifties that he married the young Elizabeth Farquarson, a Scottish lady, the daughter of General Francis Farquarson, and that in 1852 Friedrich, the first of three children, was born to them.

The first seven years of Friedrich's life were spent in Florence. In 1859 his father was transferred to the post of Austrian Minister to Belgium and here in a French civilization Friedrich remained until he was fifteen. His education in Brussels was under the direction of an eminent German Catholic historian, Baron Alfred von Reumont, who was then Prussian Minister to Belgium. During this time he was tutored by a devout Lutheran Pastor of whom he was very fond. In 1867, his father, now 72 years old, retired from the Austrian diplomatic service and came to live at Torquay in England. As a result of this European education, von Hügel was able later to carry on his correspondence with equal facility in English, French, German, or Italian, depending upon the receiver's convenience. In England, Friedrich's education was continued privately and his keen interest in the natural sciences, which had evidently come to him from his distinguished father, was strengthened by a thorough study of geology under the guidance of a Quaker, William Penegelly. This interest in geology stayed with Baron von Hügel all through his life, and his geologist's hammer was always an indispensable part of each vacation kit. In May, 1909 he wrote George Tyrrell, "I was fifty-seven yesterday and am giving myself a set of newer geological books, a geological hammer and a set of geological specimens. So expect to travel with me to gravel-pits and quarries, please."

Baron Friedrich never attended any school or university. I have never come across any comment of his own on how

he believed this to have affected him. One of the friends
who knew him best has told me how glad he was that this
highly sensitive personality, always in delicate health, but
especially so after an attack of typhus which he suffered
while at Torquay after his return from Vienna, should
never have had to suffer the standardizing pressure of a
university career, but should have been allowed to unfold
in its own natural individual way. His deafness which had
grown out of this illness increased with age and became a
real trial to him during the rest of his life. After his father's
death in 1870, von Hügel spent a year in Vienna where
he came under the spiritual training of Father Raymond
Hocking, a Dutch Dominican friar. It was during this time
on the Continent that he went through the profound religious crisis which he often refers to throughout his life.

In one of these letters to my Swedish friend where he com-
pares his own conversion with hers, and points out how
his own spiritual life, in contrast to hers, had been mediated
at each step, von Hügel wrote:

My own conversion came through or on the occasion of my
first sacramental confession when a precocious, unwholesome,
much-complicated soul of (turned) fifteen. It was deepened ap-
preciably when at eighteen by the, to me, utterly unforgettable
example, silent influence, and definite teaching of a mystically
minded but scholastically trained Dutch Dominican [Father Raymond Hocking] in Vienna when I was sickening for a typhus-
fever, when my father had just died, and when "the world" which
till then had looked so brilliant to me, turned out so distant, cold,
shallow. And the final depth attained so far was mediated for
me at forty. I felt at the time and feel still that it came straight
from God, yet on occasion of and by the help of man—by a
physically suffering, spiritually aboundingly helpful, mystical
saint, a French secular priest [Abbé Huvelin] dead now since only
a year.[4]

[4] From an unpublished letter to Emelia Fogelklou, 1910.

Almost fifty years after this youthful encounter with Father Raymond Hocking, he wrote his own niece, Gwendolyn Green, passing on to her for her own use the wise advice he had received.

When at eighteen, I made up my mind to go into moral and religious training, the great soul and mind who took me in hand —a noble Dominican—warned me—you want to grow in virtue, to serve God, to love Christ? Well you will grow in and attain to these things if you will make them a slow and sure, an utterly real, a mountain-step plod and ascent, willing to have to camp for weeks or months in spiritual desolation, darkness and emptiness at different stages in your march and growth. All demand for constant light, all attempt at eliminating or minimizing the cross and trial, is so much soft folly and puerile trifling. And what Father Hocking taught me as to spirituality is of course, also true, in its way, of all study worthy of the name.[5]

Abbé Huvelin was a French spiritual director who was attached to a small church in Paris. Through his life and humble counsel he had drawn many men from widely different walks of life into a deeper devotion to God. It was Huvelin who ministered to von Hügel in this later period of spiritual plateau that so often comes to men and women in the early forties and causes deep despair. Von Hügel again and again cites these two celibate priests and what they did and what he believed they alone could have done for him, as justification for retaining at least a celibate element in the religious institution.

In 1873 he married Lady Mary Herbert, the daughter of Sidney Herbert, Gladstone's friend and ministerial colleague. Lady Mary, following her mother's example, had joined the Roman Catholic church when she was eighteen. They settled at Hampstead where three daughters, Gertrud,

[5] *Selected Letters*, p. 266.

Hildegard, and Thekla were born to them. It was only in 1903 that they moved to Kensington Gardens where they lived until the Baron's death in 1925. In a letter written in 1904, Baron von Hügel refers to having "had altogether fully five years of Roman residence and constant touch with those behind the scenes there." [6] This knowledge of official circles in Rome was gained principally between the years of 1893 and 1902 when his wife's health compelled them to spend the winter months of each year in Italy. The memoirs of modernist colleagues like Loisy make clear how active his diplomatic work with Cardinal Rompolla and others in Rome really was in those years in behalf of their cause. After 1902, he rarely left England except for a final visit to his eldest daughter Gertrud who died of tuberculosis in Rome in August, 1915.

It was during these years before 1895 that Baron von Hügel laid much of the foundation of his broad knowledge of the sciences, of classics, of philosophy, of theology, and became one of the best critical scholars of the Bible in the Catholic church of his day. This interest had made him a friend and devoted follower of Holtzman in Germany and led to his intimate friendship with Alfred Loisy in France. His ability as a Hebrew scholar and Old Testament critic was first made generally known in a paper on "The Historical Method and the Document of the Hexateuch" which was read to the International Scientific Conference of Catholic scholars at Fribourg in 1897. It was an epoch-making innovation to present so unreservedly, as von Hügel did, the scientific historicocritical position and this occasion marked him out as a modernist leader in Catholic circles. A study in "Christology" that appeared in a French journal in 1904 indicated the penetration of his New Testament studies.

[6] *Ibid.*, p. 126.

Von Hügel and Tyrrell

In 1897 George Tyrrell's *Nova et Vetera* volume of brilliant, spiritually pointed insights into life appeared, and von Hügel was so delighted with the fresh and living appreciation of religion which he found there that he lost no time in meeting its author. The occasion had momentous consequences for them both, for they soon became the most intimate friends. Each found in the other for almost the first time someone who could begin to understand and appreciate his struggle to live, to think on, and to express his religion within the Catholic organism. With all of his characteristic generosity, the Baron was not long in opening his great learning and his cosmopolitan world to the younger Tyrrell. In 1899 Tyrrell wrote of "the strong developing influence your friendship has exerted upon my mind, in how many cases it has determined me at points of bifurcation to choose this road rather than that." It was in these years that von Hügel introduced him to Blondel and Laberthonnière, to Loisy and Duchesne and encouraged him to learn German that he might enter the world of critical studies and come to know the philosophical writings of Eucken and Troeltsch in whom the Baron was finding so much of worth.

Some feel that the great balanced mind of the Scottish-Germanic von Hügel threw too much of a critical weight upon the impetuous, swift, piercing Irish brain of Tyrrell and that his expulsion first from the Jesuit order and then after 1907 from the Roman Catholic church itself may be laid at von Hügel's door. Maude Petre calls it "a somewhat tragic friendship" and in her autobiography, her book on Loisy and her edition of the von Hügel-Tyrrell letters, she points out how if left alone George Tyrrell would have followed his natural line and made a spiritual rather than a

scientific approach to the historical problem. In this friendship she is partisan in her great adoration for Tyrrell and
is at some pains to attempt to prove that great a saint as
von Hügel was, he was not a hero martyr as her George
Tyrrell was when it came to the showdown on modernism.

It must at least be freely admitted that it was the Baron
who arranged for the translations of Tyrrell's works into
French and Italian. By this act, if by nothing more, von
Hügel was instrumental in bringing Tyrrell to the notice
of the Continental Catholic world of the authorities at
Rome as one of the most brilliant of the modernist minds,
thus marking him out for their censure. Tyrrell's tragic end
was a source of grief that never left the Baron.

In the *Selected Letters* there are twenty-seven of von
Hügel's letters to George Tyrrell and twenty-five which he
wrote to Maude Petre, who became George Tyrrell's biographer and literary executor. Among these letters the
course of the modernist controversy inside the Catholic
church can be clearly traced. But the overtones of spiritual
insight and the record of an unfolding spiritual friendship
that fill them, will in the interest of most readers, far surpass the concern with the struggle itself.

There is a dull, sickening background of wasted effort,
of spiritual mutilation, of the price of having to thwart
the disciplinary intellectual authority of the Roman Catholic
church that runs through this part of the book. The Roman
Catholic church sensing in the modernist approach a blow
at its objective foundations was harsh in its methods of
suppressing it. That the heavy hand of this authority made
of the church a purgatory for scholars, von Hügel freely
admits in his letters to Tyrrell where he confesses to the
flagellation he has himself felt, "accustomed as I am for
now well nigh thirty years, to find my friends and helpers
having to scud before the gale, or to lie low and spend a

good part of their life and strength parrying or anticipating blows." [7]

Yet in spite of his loathing for "the short-cut-and-regulations-above-all-things people," von Hügel believed that his own place was inside this great historical organism which possessed so much "depth and tenderness and heroism of Christian sanctity greater and richer than as a matter of fact is to be found elsewhere." And he begs Tyrrell again and again in these great letters toward the close of Tyrrell's life to keep his life of prayer active and to "remember the importance of having one's poor inner world to keep in order whilst fighting a larger and different world outside." [8] He wrote again later:

But I pray and hope the day may soon return when your other side, the deep mystical contemplative habit and attrait will again be so powerfully waked up and nurtured, that you will regain a grand steadiness of foundation and in your feeling as to the depths of life and of religion. With that, you will be great; without that, very unhappy. [9]

Although Tyrrell had been his best and most intimate friend, there was a growing parting of their religious opinions, although not of their personal friendship, in the last three years of Tyrrell's life. When the encyclical came in 1907, von Hügel found himself increasingly estranged from the most radical of the modernists by their growing scorn of the institutional element in religion, their leaning toward subjectivism, and their reduction of religion to a form of sheer humanitarianism. But on the central modernist demand of the right of unrestricted scientific historical criticism, von Hügel never gave in and had he been in

[7] *Ibid.*, p. 347.
[8] *Ibid.*, p. 147.
[9] *Ibid.*, p. 103.

priest's orders and hence been forced to sign the anti-modernist oath in 1910, it is difficult to see how he could have remained within the church. His status as a layman, his unimpeachable piety and loyalty to the church, his title as a Baron of the Holy Roman Empire, the fact that his wife was of an influential English family which Rome might hesitate to injure, and the well-known religious influence of von Hügel's writings upon a wider range of those outside the Catholic church than those within it, are all probably factors that shielded so prominent a modernist leader from excommunication when that party was being exterminated by every means at Rome's command.

Von Hügel As a Religious Author

It is an interesting commentary on the Baron's mind that his only two complete works, the *Mystical Element of Religion* and the *Eternal Life* were each begun as short monographs, but the richness of his learning and thought swelled them into great works in spite of his modest intention. Charles Gardiner once remarked of von Hügel that "an article to him was like holding a thimble under a full tap." Of the *Mystical Element* von Hügel wrote in the preface, "having begun to write a biography of St. Catherine with some philosophical elucidations, I have finished by writing an essay on the philosophy of mysticism illustrated by the life of Catherinetta Fiesca Adorna and her friends." [10] *Eternal Life* was begun as an article upon that subject for Dr. Hasting's *Encyclopaedia of Religion and Ethics,* but as von Hügel confesses, "I myself became so engrossed in my subject that I allowed composition to grow as long as its great subject-matter pressed it to become." [11] It was published as a separate volume in 1912.

[10] *Mystical Element of Religion,* p. xxiii.
[11] *Eternal Life,* p. v.

In order to understand his approach to religion in the letters, it is useful to notice his comment on how he was first drawn to make the preliminary study of St. Catherine of Genoa, and later to use her as a biographical illustration out of whose rich character he could make this unsurpassed study of the mystical element in the life of religion. There was first of all, a practical attraction in that the texts of St. Catherine's life needed scrupulous untangling, and with his taste for this work whetted by much critical work on scriptural and classical tests, he was eager to attempt it. It may be mentioned incidentally that he did for the texts of St. Catherine much what Sabatier in his studies had done for those of St. Francis of Assisi. But there were deeper attractions. It was in Catherine of Genoa that he found a figure who had lived in an atmosphere of prereformation, nonmilitarized Catholicism which always impressed the Baron as the golden age, as the approximation of Catholicism at anything like its highest form. He also found in St. Catherine's life an illustration of all sides of the mystical life both in its greatness and in its profound difficulties and dangers. But most of all, he wanted to study and find how a soul that had developed so great a taste for the Infinite could still make room for the historical, the institutional, and the intellectual elements in her religious life. He found all of this in Catherine of Genoa and he found it in a saint who had lived the common life, who had married, who had found a great religious reality and who had devoted her life to the humble service of the poor and sick, and all of this quite outside any formal religious order. Here for von Hügel was supreme creatureliness buoyed up by and in contact with the Divine, and here awaiting him was the task of interpreting the problems of mysticism in the study of so attractive a character.

Baron von Hügel wrote Tyrrell in 1898 that he was nearly

two-thirds finished with his biography of St. Catherine, but as the work grew from the original purpose of a hundred and twenty page monograph to two rich volumes of nearly eight times that length, von Hügel labored on and it was not until 1908 when he was fifty-six years old that it was first published. The *Mystical Element of Religion* was more than a mere work of great scholarship. It could more nearly be described as a spiritual autobiography, for of this work, Baron von Hügel wrote in the opening lines of the preface: "it embodies well nigh all the writer has been able to LEARN AND TO TEST, for the matter of religion during now some thirty years of adult life." [12]

Baron von Hügel's style, both in his letters and his books, is like that of no one else. It is electrified with his own personality. There are in places, especially in the *Mystical Element,* truly ponderous sections which one must severely concentrate upon in order to get at his meaning. But there are also passages and phrases of the most brilliant eloquence. To have overcome the fact that, as he admits, fully seven-tenths of his reading and much of his thinking were done in German, and to have written as lucid an English style as he has, is the real miracle to consider. Each of von Hügel's sentences seems to have been so carefully weighed and qualified in order for it to express the whole truth of the matter at hand, that it *does* at times have the appearance of being, as Tyrrell accused him, "stuffed like a tight sausage. Solid, liquid, gas—are the three forms in which thought can be presented," and, Tyrrell went on to remind him, "the last is for an audience, the second for a book, the first for an archangel in retreat." [13] The later essays and letters show a marked improvement in the style with which the Baron expressed the richness of his thought.

[12] *Mystical Element,* p. xxi.
[13] *Selected Letters,* p. 13.

The first volume of *Essays and Addresses on the Philosophy of Religion* appeared in 1921 and was made up principally of papers given to different societies which had begun to besiege him with requests to lecture to them after the appearance of the *Mystical Element* had made him well known in England outside Catholic circles. In these years his best thought had been poured into these addresses and perhaps even more fully into his huge correspondence.

"A Missionary of Christianity to the Intellects of Men"

Among his correspondents and friends in Germany, there was Troeltsch and Eucken, Holtzman and Heiler; in Sweden, Archbishop Söderblom; in Italy, his many modernist friends and admirers like Murri until the estrangement after 1908; in France there was Loisy, Blondel, Laberthonnière, Brémond and until his death, of course, his beloved Abbé Huvelin. In England, until the Synthetic Society dissolved in 1908, he was in constant touch with men like Arthur Balfour, Bishop Talbot and Bishop Gore, Lord Haldane, James Bryce, Edward Dicey, Dr. Martineau, R. H. Hutton, James Ward and Henry Sidgwick of Cambridge, and Dr. Rashdall.

His *intimate* friends in England outside of George Tyrrell were in no way limited to Catholics. Canon A. L. Lilley; Professor C. C. J. Webb, 'the Philosophical Anglican' as von Hügel affectionately termed him; D. A. Claude Montefiore, Professor Percy Gardiner; Mrs. Stuart Moore, better known as Evelyn Underhill, and in his last years perhaps most of all, Professor Norman Kemp-Smith of Edinburgh, were very close to him. His constant communication with thought in all the European centers drew Maude Petre in her *Life of George Tyrrell* to refer to the Baron as "one who had done more than any man living to bring together the pro-

foundest religious thinkers of the age." [14] And the great
ecumenical Swedish Protestant leader, Nathan Söderblom,
confirms this in observing that "no other man in our age has,
as far as I can see, become a teacher and an initiator to
seeking and believing souls in all the chief sections of the
entire Church and Communion of Christ, as von Hügel." [15]
Is it any wonder then that Loisy called him "a missionary
of Christianity to the intellects of men?"

In 1922, he accepted the election to the Gifford lectureship for 1924–25, perhaps the highest honor which the
Anglo-Saxon world can bestow upon a philosopher or religious thinker. A break in his delicate health, however,
prevented either his completion of the lectures or his de-
livery of any of them. The subject of them was to have been
"The Reality of God" and on this great subject von Hügel
felt he was to make his most important contribution to
religion. He was dictating to his secretary portions of this
book up to the day before his death in January 1925.
When he knew that he was dying and that he must leave
unfinished these lectures that were so dear to him, he said
quietly, "I shall live it out in the beyond." The uncom-
pleted lectures were published in 1928 under the title of
the *Reality of God*. A second volume of *Collected Essays
and Addresses on the Philosophy of Religion* was post-
humously published in 1926 and the following year Bernard
Holland's handsome biographical memoir was included in
his edition of the *Selected Letters of Baron Friedrich von
Hügel*. It is in these letters that one can best approach the
great humanity and religious depth of soul of this "self-
spending" servant of God.

It was in the London Society for the Study of Religion

[14] Maude Petre, *Life of George Tyrrell* (London: Arnold, 1912), II,
p. 87.
[15] *Selected Letters*, p. 53.

that Baron von Hügel was perhaps seen and his influence felt most constantly during the last twenty years of his life, for he had been an enthusiastic member of the Society from the time of its founding in 1903. The Society, composed of men drawn in certain fixed proportions from the different religious bodies, had exactly that tolerant breadth of religious understanding with which the Baron was always in deepest sympathy. Dr. Gow of Manchester College, Oxford, has often told me of the Baron's way of criticizing a paper in the Society. Being deaf he was always given the paper to study over in advance. When he rose to comment, he would first find the best in the paper and express most warmly his appreciation of it. "That's fine!" "Ah! that was so fine, I thought," "How much I like that," "How true *that* is" were favorite expressions of his. But after this, Dr. Gow insisted, there was no one in the Society who could probe with so gentle a kindness and yet with so firm and penetrating a clarity to the difficulties involved. "No, no this won't do at all."

In his letters, his approach was the same. There is always appreciation, even affection and gratitude for the positive things in the writer. He gives a clue to his approach in a letter to a friend: "If it is not enthusiasm and enthusiastic sympathy—of course only for what we see is true and fruitful—that makes men grow and advance in all things, then I should like to be told what it is." Then comes as searching a criticism as could be had, but in conclusion there is usually again "but what a meanster I am to carp at any part of so helpful, fine a book!" [16]

The Givenness of God

Like Francis de Sales, Baron von Hügel's direction of souls which we must now turn to for the balance of our

[16] *Selected Letters*, p. 171.

examination of his work, grew out of his view of the nature of religion and of the way in which a soul should be guided in order to encourage its most complete development into a divinely-centered life.

Von Hügel, especially during the latter part of his life, emphasized the givenness, the prevenience, the ever-present reality, the over-againstness of God. He loved to quote the lines from Bernard of Clairvaux:

Do you awake? Well, He, too, is awake. If you rise in the night-time, if you anticipate to your utmost your earliest awaking, you will already find Him waking—you will never anticipate His own awakeness. In such an intercourse you will always be rash if you attribute any priority and predominant share to yourself; for He loves both more than you, and before you love at all."

And in his own words he expresses this, "God not only loves us more and better than we can ever love ourselves . . . but God loved us before we loved, or could love, Him. God's love of us rendered possible and actual our love of God." [17] It is Pascal with a variant, "You would not have sought Me if I had not already sought you."

In his own fine essay on *Prayer* von Hügel devotes the first part to "Facts and Doctrines Concerning God," and only in the second part does he deal with man's side in "Facts and Truths Concerning the Soul." That the sequence is significant to him comes out again when he congratulated C. C. J. Webb upon the occasion of his Gifford Lectures thanking him for the priority that he used in devoting the first volume to God, and the second to Personality in his "God and Personality" series. There is no reducing this transcendence, this priority of God to any subjectively exhaustible terms. Rather we must become aware of what

[17] *Essays and Addresses* (2nd ser.), p. 224.

on all levels of our life lures us on. In describing to a conference, in 1917, the nature of his own conversion experience, he insists that it was "the successfully awakening me to the fact of deep reality encompassing me on every side that saved me." [18] Again he writes in a letter to Mrs. Lillie: "Now Religion begins with a full affirmation of a Reality, of a Reality other than and more than all mankind. . . . It is a gift from above downwards, not a groping from below upwards. It is not like Science, a coral-reel, it is more like a golden shower from above." [19]

This clear realistic approach that broke with idealism and subjectivism and which moved sharply away from psychologizing and depicting God as deducible from human selfhood or any of man's own powers has had a deep and lasting influence on English religious thought. I once heard Canon Streeter wisely observe that Barthianism would never have the vogue in England that it had had on the Continent since von Hügel had already done its principal constructive work of restoring the transcendent aspect of God, but that he had done it in such a sound way that England might be spared so many of the fantastic Barthian extravagances that the Continent would have to unlearn afterward!

This view of God's prevenience, always directed von Hügel's instruction of those who would learn to pray. "Our prayer will certainly gain in depth and aliveness, if we thus continually think of God as the true inspirer of our most original-seeming thoughts and wishes, whensoever these are good and fruitful—as Him who secretly initiates, what He openly crowns." [20]

Always in first place in von Hügel's instruction on prayer

[18] *Selected Letters*, p. 64.
[19] *Ibid.*, p. 353.
[20] *Essays and Addresses* (2nd ser.) , p. 225.

is the prayer of adoration. "The first and central act of religion is adoration, sense of God" he wrote to his niece.[21] He went so far as to tell Mrs. Cecil Chapman that "Religion is Adoration." For to become aware of the prevenient grace of God is to long to answer that love in lifting up the heart to Him. And with this realization and this answering back comes a glad sense of "creatureliness"—a favorite expression of von Hügel's.

His personal testimony of his own need, his own dependence upon, and his own response to this prior love of God is given in an unforgettable way in his confessions to two dear relations of his, J. M. and his niece. To J. M., as a young girl, he wrote:

The fact is that the poor thing that scribbles these lines is *the work of religion*. I weigh my words, Child: I should not be physically alive at this moment; I should be, were I alive at all, a corrupt or at least an incredibly unhappy, bitter, self-occupied destructive soul were it not for religion—for its having come and saved me from myself—it and nothing else; it in place of everything else, it, in a sense even against everything else . . . and by religion I mean not some vague sentiment or some beautiful thought, not even, though this is getting nearer to it, moral striving as apart from faith in, and realization of, the great Spiritual Reality, God, in Whose presence, and as Whose will, we thus strive to grow and be: but by and in self donation, such self-commitment to a, to *the* Reality other than, yet immensely near to ourselves.[22]

To his niece he confides, "Without religion, I should have been unbearable—I needed it to water me down." [23] And again "We are not God. Yet how we need Him! And this

[21] *Selected Letters*, p. 251.
[22] *Ibid.*, pp. 189, 194.
[23] Gwendolyn Green, *F. Hügel's Letters to a Niece* (New York: E. P. Dutton & Co., Inc., 1928).

then not as just a larger ourselves, not as a larger becoming, but as Being, as Joy, Pure and Undefiled." [24]

Von Hügel's Treatment of Suffering

One of the most searching tests that can be set to the ultimate adequacy of any philosophy is to note how it teaches its followers to face suffering. In von Hügel it is against this background of God's ever-present, joyous initiative in loving us and in bearing us up, that he gives his instruction on how a Christian may face and actually use suffering to grow in the life of God. Here again the Baron spoke out of a deep personal reservoir of experience and the authentic note is present about all that he suggests on this subject. To a friend in her last illness, he wrote four letters on suffering that might form a classic on the subject. There is no shallow denial of its existence, but a frank facing of the cause of the mental rebellion against the meaningless-ness of suffering, as well as the dealing with suffering itself.

I have long felt that it is *the apparent sterility of suffering* which adds the final trial to our pains; and that this appearance (of its sterility) is *most truly* only an appearance. No, of course I do not mean that suffering simply of itself is good or operates good; but that God is more living and real than all suffering and all sin; and that He can and will, and does give concomitant opportunities and graces and growths to the sufferer, if and when the latter is humble, watchful and prayerful in such utilizations.[25]

The next letter contains my own favorite passage in von Hügel on the subject of suffering:

How wonderful it is, is it not, that literally only Christianity has taught us the true peace and function of suffering. The Stoics tried the hopeless little game of denying its objective real-

[24] *Selected Letters*, p. 331.
[25] *Ibid.*, p. 127.

ity, or of declaring it a good in itself (which it never is), and the Pessimists tried to revel in it as a food to their melancholy and as something that can no more be transformed than it can be avoided or explained. But Christ came and He did not really explain it; He did far more, He met it, willed it, transformed it, and He taught us how to do all this, or rather He himself does it within us, if we do not hinder His all-healing hands. Pray for us all, even just in passing, please. In suffering we are very near to God [26]

and he signed himself, "Your affectionate old friend."

His third and fourth letters get down to specifics and they are passed on as from one scarred veteran to another:

As to your spiritual question, my dear—, as to how you are, not simply, once for all, at the beginning of all this discomfort and pain, to accept and will it; but (as you most rightly feel, a very different thing) how you are to stand it, to keep on accepting it, day by day, even hour by hour, possibly minute by minute (I mean, as to the proximity of pain to pain, and weakness to weakness) : let me suggest to you the following. I take it that *this is precisely the most irreplaceable function and grace of suffering,* when it is at all at its fullest that we cannot, do what we will, cut a decent figure in our own eyes; that it rises, *emphatically,* beyond a stoic exercise. All we can then do (and how dear and darling this poor little "all" is then to God!) is gently to drop, gently to try to drop, all foresight whatsoever; to treat the question how we are going to stand this for a month, or a week, or a day, or even an hour, as a little presumption on our part. We cannot really, or ourselves, "stand" it properly, for half an hour; and God will and does give us His grace to stand it, for as long as ever He chooses, provided we will, according to the intensity of the trial, contract our outlook, to the day, or the hour, or even the minute. God, the essentially timeless, will thus and then help His poor timeful creature to contract time to a point of most fruitful faith and love.[27]

[26] *Ibid.,* p. 228.
[27] *Ibid.,* pp. 230–31.

Try more and more *at the moment itself*, without any delay or evasion, without any fixed form, as simply, as spontaneously as possible, to cry out to God, to Christ our Lord, in any way that comes most handy, and the more variously the better. "Oh! Oh! this is real: oh! deign to accept it, as a little real atonement for real sin!" "Oh, help me to move on, from finding pain so real, to discovering sin to be far more real." "Oh, may this pang deepen me, may it help to make me real, real—really humble, really loving, really ready to live or die with my soul in Thy hands". . . And so on, and so on. You could end by such ejaculations costing your *brain* practically nothing. The all-important point is, to make them *at the time* and *with the pain well mixed up into the prayer*.[28]

To his niece whom he is initiating into the mature spiritual world, he gathers all of this up in saying:

. . . to suffer well is far more difficult than to act well (although the ordinary talk is that we have just "to grin and bear" suffering —we can do nothing to it or with it!!!) Holy suffering is the very crown of holy action. And God is no pedant: He can and does look to the substance of our suffering, and knows how to penetrate beyond our surface restlessness or murmurs. Indeed, part of the great work suffering effects in the soul doubtless springs from the way in which, when acute, it almost invariably humbles us: we can much less easily cut a fine figure in our own eyes over our sufferings, than we can over our actions when in peace and plenty.

You understand all the above completely, I trust? We will both do what gently, peaceably we can to have all our Purgatory —every drop of it—here; and then Heaven, the closest union, unfailing, with Pure Joy, with All Purity, with Christ, with God.[29]

In writing to Gladstone's daughter upon the occasion of her father's death, von Hügel says: "There is surely for us

28 *Ibid.*, p. 231.
29 *Ibid.*, p. 340.

Christians, no surer test of Faith on our part, nor truer
proof of Love on God's part, than suffering nobly borne,
. . . and nothing that unites and reunites like suffering.
. . . I have always loved to think of devoted suffering as
the highest, purest, perhaps the only quite pure form of
action." [30] One of von Hügel's most treasured sayings of
Abbé Huvelin was his remark, "Sanctity and suffering, they
are one and the same thing. You will never be able really
to help others except through suffering, only by suffering.
Our Lord laid hold of the world, not by fine speeches, not
by the Sermon on the Mount, but by His blood, His suffering on the cross." [31]

Fastidiousness and Christian Creatureliness

To his niece again he commends the lesson of that funda-
mental Christian doctrine "creatureliness" in regard to
Christianity's renunciation of fastidiousness:

Its [Christianity's] greatness, its special genius, consists, as
much as in anything else, in that it is without this fastidiousness.
A soul that is, I do not say tempted, but dominated, by such
fastidiousness, is as yet only hovering round the precincts of
Christianity, but it has not entered its sanctuary, where heroism
is always homely, where the best always acts as stimulus towards
helping, towards being (in a true sense) but one of the semi-
articulate, bovine, childish, repulsively second-third-fourth-rate
crowd. So it was with Jesus Himself; so it was with St. Francis,
the Poverello; so it is with every soul that has fully realized the
genius of the Christian paradox. When I told you of my choking
emotion in reading, St. John's Gospel, that scene of Jesus, the
Light of the World (that He is this, is an historic fact), as the
menial servant at the feet of those foolish little fishermen and
tax-gatherers, what do you think moves me but just that huge

[30] *Ibid.*, p. 70.
[31] *Ibid.*, p. 62.

life-and-love-bringing paradox, here in its fullest activity? The heathen Philosophies, one and all, failed to get beyond your fastidiousness; only Christianity got beyond it; only Christianity —but I mean, a deeply *costingly* realized Christianity—got beyond it. It is really, a very hideous thing; the full, truly free, beauty of Christ alone completely liberates us from this miserable bondage.[32]

He implemented this, as his niece recalled, by suggesting to anyone who asked him for advice: "Could you manage to visit the poor?" A little before his death he is reported to have said, "Christianity taught us to care. Caring is the greatest thing in the world, caring is all that matters."

Once more to this beloved niece whom he apparently knows has a heavy chore of packing ahead of her, he writes an affectionate letter on the creaturely response to whatever God sends her, on what Caussade calls "the sacrament of the present moment," on taking what is at hand and making of it a holy work for Him:

True, certain other acts, at other moments, will be wanted, of a kind more intrinsically near to God—Prayer, Quiet, Holy Communion. Yet not even these other acts could unite you as closely to God as can do this packing, if and when the packing is the duty of certain moments, and if, and as often as, the little old daughter does this her packing with her heart and intention turned to God her Home, if she offers her packing as her service, that service which is perfect liberty.

Not even a soul already in Heaven, not even an angel or archangel, can take your place there; for what God wants, what God will love to accept, in those rooms, in those packing days, and from your packing hands, will be just this little packing performed by you in those little rooms. Certainly it has been mainly through my realizing this doctrine a little, and through my poor little self-exercising in it, that I have got on a bit, and you will

[32] *Ibid.*, p. 258.

get on faster than I have done with it. You understand? At one moment, packing; at another, silent adoration in Church; at another, dreariness and unwilling drift; at another, the joys of human affections given and received; at another, keen, keen suffering of soul, of mind, in apparent utter loneliness; at another, external acts of religion; at another, death itself. All these occupations every one can, ought, and will be, each when and where, duty, reason, conscience, necessity—God—calls for it; it will all become the means and instruments of loving, of transfiguration, of growth for your soul, and of its beatitude. But it is for God to choose these things, their degrees, combinations, successions; and it is for you just simply, very humbly, very gently and peacefully, to follow that leading.[33]

Home Remedies for Inward Dryness

The same note of creatureliness, of being willing to recognize this abiding caring of God over against our own earthiness that will so often obscure our view of Him and leave us in the pitch darkness of spiritual dryness and of despair, marks the instructions which he passes on to his niece to help her to deal with these periods of inward poverty.

Let me give you three images, all of which have helped me on along "many a flinty furlong." At eighteen I learnt from Father Raymond Hocking, that grandly interior-minded Dominican, that I certainly could, with God's grace, give myself to Him, and strive to live my life-long with Him and for Him. But that this would mean winning and practising much desolation—that I would be climbing a mountain where, off and on, I might be enveloped in mist for days on end, unable to see a foot before me. Had I noticed how mountaineers climb mountains? How they have a quiet, regular, short step—on the level it looks petty; but then this step they keep up, on and on as they ascend, whilst the inexperienced townsman hurries along, and soon has to stop,

[33] *Ibid.*, p. 287.

dead beat with the climb. That such an expert mountaineer, when the thick mists come, halts and camps out under some slight cover brought with him, quietly smoking his pipe, and moving on only when the mist has cleared away.

Then in my thirties I utilized another image, learnt in my Jesuit Retreats. How I was taking a long journey on board ship with great storms pretty sure ahead of me; and how I must now select, and fix in my little cabin, some few but entirely appropriate things—a small trunk fixed up at one end, a chair that would keep its position, tumbler and glass that would do ditto: all this, simple, strong, and selected throughout in view of stormy weather. So would my spirituality have to be chosen and cultivated, especially in view of "dirty" weather.

And lastly, in my forties another image helped me—they all three are in pretty frequent use still!—I am travelling on a camel across a huge desert. Windless days occur and then all is well. But hurricanes of wind will come, unforeseen, tremendous. What to do then? It is very simple, but it takes much practice to do well at all. Dismount from the camel, fall prostrate face downwards on the sand, covering your head with your cloak. And lie thus, an hour, three hours, half a day; the sand storm will go, and you will arise, and continue your journey as if nothing had happened. The old Uncle has had many, many such sand storms. How immensely useful they are! [34]

It would be hard to find more staple counsel than these three figures provide to help guide one through times of inner dryness.

The Three Elements of Religion

The other aspect of von Hügel's view of the nature of religion which lay behind the spiritual counsel which his letters give was his sense of religion's breadth. The only appropriate response of a man to the divine initiative is a whole response—one that will call for his whole nature

[34] *Ibid.*, pp. 304-5.

which means the habit-life of his will, the full thrust of his intellect, and the total response of his emotions. If he withholds any one of these from responding to God, his religion will be an impoverished one.

The first of these features, the habit-life of the will, von Hügel connects with the institutional or historical side of religion, and no one in our time has done more to interpret the significance of the social, institutional aspect of religion than von Hügel. We are not self-made. We are born into a family. We receive our language, our primitive expectations and obligations, our very heroes from the nurture of the group. We are compelled to draw upon the deposits of others in this precious bank every day of our lives. Therefore there must be a bank to carry over to us the gifts of the spiritual insights of ages past. And here the Christian church furnishes us such a residuary. It brings the Christian past to each fresh individual. It confronts the spontaneous but limited immediate experience of each individual with the enduring experience of the great souls who have gone before him. It preserves and turns over to him his heritage of the Bible, of liturgy, of the saints and of holy lives and, by crossing these with his own immediate spontaneous experience, it draws his life into the great broad stream of Christian response to God.

Never has religion been purely and entirely individual; always it has been as truly and necessarily social and institutional, traditional and historical. And this traditional element, not all the religious genius in the world can ever escape or replace: it was there surrounding and molding the very pre-natal existence of each of us; it will be there long after we have left the scene. We live and die its wise servants, or its blind slaves, or in futile impoverishing revolt against it: we never for good or for evil really get beyond its reach.[35]

[35] *Mystical Element*, I, p. 59.

Von Hügel knew his own and his fellow's weaknesses and faced them with his characteristic frankness. We are creatures of short memories. We are easily engrossed in the secular life of our time. There must be a towering witness to the supernatural world in the midst of the natural and secular calling men back to God, an "awakening of souls to, the preparing them for, the *other* life, the life beyond the grave." The Church was such a witness, such a reminder. It is a sheet anchor for our souls in any storm we may meet. Letter after letter to his niece interprets this historical and institutional aspect of the religious life to her. "How I should love it," he writes to her affectionately, "if in times to come, I knew you ran into Church in any joy or sorrow."

Much as he loved the Roman Catholic church, von Hügel showed great tolerance of other sects and religions than his own. He would have approved of Maude Petre's remark counseling the importance of rooting yourself in some branch of the Christian church, "But just because there are so many possible roads through time and eternity, do we need to choose one road; just because of the vastness of life, do we need a shelter." [36]

There was little of the proselytizer to Rome in von Hügel. As completely convinced as he was of the richness of the Roman Catholic church, he knew well the terrible jar for one reared as a Protestant which the church's heavy, gloved hand of authority would impose upon him. He might as readily have said to an aspirant for membership in the Roman Catholic church, what he remarked to a friend about the Jesuit Society, "Upon God, I owe my salvation to the Jesuits, but don't you have anything to do with them." Yet the religious life that is not imbedded in some institutional organism is destined to be infinitely the poorer for it.

[36] Maude Petre, *My Way of Faith* (New York: E. P. Dutton & Co., Inc., 1937), p. xxv.

A second element of the religious life which is of equal importance was the intellectual, the scientific side of life. He saw that thought must be given a free rein to follow out truth by its own standards, and his whole struggle as a modernist was connected with regaining this freedom for Catholic scholars as they had once possessed it in the golden day of Nicholas of Cusa. He believed that if one were firmly attached to the center one could be very free at the periphery.

He had an exceptionally fruitful notion of the modern abstract, critical-historical and physical sciences as a kind of modern form of asceticism, in which all of one's subjective emotional and private biases were dispassionately set aside before this objective inquiry, and he recommended that all who would give themselves to the religious life should have some scientific field in which to experience the ego-cleansing power of such an utterly dispassionate, abstract endeavor. His geology and his own textual criticism had given him an experience of its worth.

He wrote George Tyrrell:

Every man ought to be trained in retreats that he must study or work at something definite and concrete . . . because without this, he will, as we know and see things, neglect one of the two twin means of growing lowly and pure and of removing himself from the center of his (otherwise little) world . . . experimental science and criticism act still more efficiently in this direction (as a clearer of the eye, as a purification of the heart).[37]

He saw, too, that the critical intellect must be continually free to examine the religious life: its content, its institutional claims to authority, its relation to the other interests of life. And he saw also that unless the intellect freely criticized religion, punctured its superstitions, and helped

[37] *Von Hügel and Tyrrell,* pp. 35–40.

to guide its development wisely, that religion could soon stale and atrophy and that high religion would soon become low religion.

For von Hügel, however, not only the habit-life of the will and the active life of the intellect must be operative in religion, but the whole emotional and feeling life of a man as well. And it is in this firsthand experience of the presence of God that is called the mystical element of religion that von Hügel was especially at home. This was the source, this the renewer, this the goal of the religious life. And his own practice of prayer, his regular daily quarter of an hour of devotional reading which he so carefully describes in the letters, his examination of conscience, his daily intercessions, now for Tyrrell: "I can most truthfully declare that no day passes, but you are at least thrice in my prayers," and now for a beloved family whom he assures that he has prayed for three times a day for forty years—these were all a part and parcel of his own response to this mystical firsthand side which is so central in all religion. Five persons in his generation helped to recover the preciousness of this mystical tradition for the Anglo-Saxon world: William James, Dean Inge, Rufus M. Jones, Evelyn Underhill and the Baron himself. But the intense souls whom these writers tended to exalt, von Hügel always maintained were only the articulators of a common hidden life in every soul, and it was of this common emotional life that he spoke in describing this element of religion.

There is no pitting of one of these elements as static over against another as dynamic in von Hügel, as Bergson was to do in his *Two Sources of Morality and Religion*. The life of religion, which von Hügel taught in his letters, was always one where the rich friction of all three of these elements was operative. "The essence, too, of all religion, and of Our Lord's teaching and spirit in particular, is not to be sought in one element, but in the underlying linkage and interaction of them all" [38] he wrote Percy Gardiner.

If any element is omitted an impoverishment or perversion results. He pointed out how sects that leave out the historical and institutional side and attempt to live purely on their own immediate spiritual experiences were trying to live on glacier water and almost inevitably become shallow and self-righteous and after a few decades or centuries wither away. Those churches who admit the institutional and intellectual but are fearful of the mystical life tend to become coldly moralistic and lose all fervor. Of individuals who often show the same traits as religious groups, he wrote, "Many of those who are entirely right on the dry critical side of things, have nothing and will know nothing of what I am convinced is its corrective and supplement, mystical aspiration and action." [39] Those churches which exalt the institutional and mystical, but who fear and seek to root out the intellectual life tend to become fanatical, narrow-minded and superstitious. They lose the intellect's power of purifying criticism which can call them back to the divine tension, balance and proportion. It is alone by giving not one or two but all three of these elements free play that the full religious life is to be built. It is discovered only in the tension, the interaction, the difficult blending, the divine friction of all of these elements held in working relationship in a single life.

He lived as he taught. In writing of her uncle, Gwendolyn Green says in *Two Witnesses:*

But though we see in him very clearly the touch of the mystical being, yet he was not so peculiarly mystical as immensely rich; he contrives to contain within himself to an almost unique degree, a fragment of all the three elements that man's religious nature

[38] *Selected Letters,* p. 112.
[39] *Ibid.,* p. 82.

requires for its fullest growth. . . . He is active, intellectual *and* mystical—neither of the three alone; so he spoke of all three in conjunction, and did not dwell on one.[40]

It is good to close these discussions of devotional books with the *Letters* of Friedrich von Hügel. For after almost twenty years of close and affectionate touch with his *Letters* and with his other writings, I can testify that he wears well. He saw the religious life as a life of devotion that should be entered upon for the long pull. "And certainly it is perseverance in the spiritual life, on and on across the years and the changes of our moods and trials, health and environment; it is this that supremely matters." [41] He might well have added to this "perseverance on and on across the years," the phrase "and on across the span of eternity as well," for the message of his life, as of his letters, bore out the old maxim, that in the life of devotion—there are no vacations either here or hereafter.

[40] *Two Witnesses,* p. 143.
[41] *Selected Letters,* p. 290.